Out of the Ordinary:
Politics, Poetry and Narrative

Gary Geddes

Mackie Lecture and Reading Series, No. 6

Cover design by Christine McPhee and Kalamalka Press.

© Kalamalka Press and Gary Geddes

Published in 2009 by The Kalamalka Press, An imprint of the Kalamalka Institute for Working Writers, of Okanagan College, 7000 College Way, Vernon, BC, V1B 2N5, Canada

The Kalamalka Press Board of Directors is Frances Greenslade, James Hamilton, John Lent, Craig McLuckie and Ross Tyner.

Production and Editing on this volume by Craig McLuckie, Frances Greenslade, John Lent, Jake Kennedy and Ross Tyner.

Library and Archives Canada Cataloguing in Publication

Geddes, Gary, 1940-
    Out of the ordinary: politics, poetry and narrative / Gary Geddes.

(Mackie lecture and reading series ; 6)
ISBN 978-0-9738057-8-9

    I. Title. II. Series: Mackie lecture and reading series 6

PS8563.E3O88 2009   C814'.54   C2009-905657-7

Cover Illustration: Garden of Opposites, Martin Honisch.
Author photograph: Danielle Schaub

Printed in Canada, under the capable direction of Mr. Harry van Asseldonk, by Okanagan College Print Services, Kelowna.

Contents

A Long Note on G.G.'s *Out of the Ordinary: Politics, Poetry and Narrative*

"Who remembers names or issues now?"
—Gary Geddes, "Standard Bearer" from *The Terracotta Army*

- Just get out of the way for G. and this; for 'this' being these voices of history; for (the dedication/to) memory; for (never against) the ordinary; for the dissident poet-citizen; for that which refuses to be party to and instead opts relentlessly "to bear witness;" for (like) famous Seamus: poetry is "a glimpsed alternative, a revelation of potential that is denied or constantly threatened by circumstances" and because G. believes in poetry's *giving*-power; for the unfashionable idea of poetry as an expansion of the human; for (thus) the important place of the long poem — as a potentiality: to know/develop individual, regional and national identities; for a politics of the national that recognizes that "Canadian poets first have to overcome certain false notions about the country, perpetrated by government, vested interests, and educational institutions committed to maintaining the status quo" (we are not peacemakers or -keepers!); for, moreover, G.'s declaration that "There is nothing literary that the long poem should not be able to do; it needn't surrender its powers to the drama or the short story or the novel, just because those forms are currently in favour with the reading public and academia, or because a group of contemporary poets has lost both its powers of narrative and its belief in character and community"; for the phrase 'the perfect reciprocity' not as instantiating tidy equivalencies but as privileging the sacrifice of self to other... and art's longing to meet that ideal; for, as G. puts it, "To make these moments of our history *strong enough to be remembered*, the poet needs all the resources of language at his [her] disposal, just as he needs to put all his own psychic and intellectual resources at the disposal of the language, in a perfect reciprocity"; for a poetics therefore of the responsible; for how such a poetics battles against the ironic and the trite; for how to use poetry, then, to arm the spirit; for G.'s magic erudition that ranges from quotes from steelworkers to philosophers to the Palestinian poet Jabra Ibrahim Jabra: "As the sciences take over in the organization of society, the poet's intuition may not be heeded so much, but it remains operative at a certain level in the collective life where society finds nourishment, if not actual salvation, in its secret dreams. The poet thus remains an unexpected determinant of action, a motivator of change"; for the limpid fact in G. that poetry *does* make something happen; for the verdict that language may be reclaimed from our 'post-literate' age and, indeed, that poetry—being in its core *about* recall—is ideally equipped for such radical recoveries; for a recognition that aesthetics may never be entirely separated from ideology/that is, that all aesthetics being ideological it behoves the contemporary artist to labour at a poetry of beautiful justice; for being at home equally with EJ Pratt and bpnichol and honouring the distinct drive to narrate in both: "What we have [in nichol's *Continental Trance*], instead of the building of the railway, is the construction of tracks of language, not just the poetic main-line, but trunk-lines, branch-lines of meaning, drawn from a playful mind using associative logic: 'notation / in the landscape of a nation & / a revelation'; for the courage to be against the fad-ism of the negative and so also-for the seeking out of an alternative experimental ground but on terms of the human; for belief; for a bold stand against the loss of caring as a universal; for G.'s poetry being not one of refusals but one of offerings; for a kind of essayistic sound that is more passionate talk than desiccated dissertating: "Poetry, too, is made from gifts, not refusals. Its existence in the life of our society depends upon its ability to absorb and assimilate new materials (linguistic and otherwise), to take upon itself the widest possible range of information, idea, event, theme"; for the modesty of address: these words want to be read (the purest gift); for the table of contents itself as ethico-poetic map: reciprocations, unities, endurance, desire, bridgings, witness (most especially witness); for the echoes of those silenced ones; for poetry as serious song and serious dance and serious play; for the truth that, like American poet Susan Howe's declaration that "I wish I could tenderly lift from the dark side of history, voices that are anonymous, slighted—inarticulate," G. too believes (and states) that "All poetry, whether narrative, descriptive, lyrical, meditative, documentary or imagistic, is someone's story. The words we use and the feelings that produce them constitute our story and are coloured by what we are and what we know. In the case of very fine poets, though, the story takes on the character and proportions of myth and becomes not just someone else's story, but our own, the story of us all;" for all of this.

Jake Kennedy, Kelowna, September 2009

Introduction
Gary Geddes

Putting together these disparate essays was prompted by two events. The first was an invitation to serve as writer-in-residence at the Mackie House in Vernon, initiated by Okanagan College. I spent two enjoyable weeks in an elegant old estate in the company of a large cat named Persephone. One of the responsibilities that this largesse laid on my shoulders was to begin work on something that might be published by Kalamalka Press. As I was thoroughly immersed in plans to travel to sub-Saharan Africa to research a book on human rights tentatively called *Bright Sun, Dark Shadow*, I pondered the advisability of bringing together in book form some of my disparate essays and talks. Several of these pieces had been composed as keynote addresses, at the request of universities and organizations. A few had been published in remote journals.

The second event that prompted me to reconsider the matter was the Prime Minister's decision to cut spending to certain cultural programs, especially Canadian artists abroad, and his unfortunate characterization of Canadian writers as hopelessly out of touch with the lives and needs of 'ordinary' Canadians. Much of my writing, whether in the form of poetry or non-fiction, had been directed to so-called ordinary Canadians, creative people who care about their country and the state of the world they live in: farming relatives, a bricklayer, a commercial fisherman, a mechanic, a psychologist, a truck driver father and an indefatigable stepmother who managed to raise a family, pack tins of salmon at the cannery in Steveston and inspire her sons to work hard and aim high. I never doubted the creativity of these people, whose imaginative acts, including the telling of stories and the playing of instruments, brought moments of joy and laughter into our otherwise very modest existence.

As I looked over the various pieces, I noticed certain preoccupations: history, memory, political engagement and how to be in this world, how to love place and heritage, but to love the planet and its cultural and natural diversity even more. I was surprised by some of my passionate pronouncements in these sketchy, impressionistic talks. I had proposed that Canada needs a new naming; that one of the writer's tasks is to challenge things as they are; that micro-history—what often falls between the cracks—has more to offer than the sloppy but comfortable master narratives we like to wrap ourselves in. I saw that much of my time had been spent sharing my interest in and admiration for the long poem in all its manifestations, as narrative, as poem-sequence, as quasi-documentary, as sustained meditation. The long poem, for me as a writer, has been, obviously, a kind of home-place, a terrain where I could take a deep breath, stretch my wings and explore big subjects, ideas as bold and brash and unwieldy as Canada itself.

So I thought, why not let these pieces stand as a companion volume to *Letters from Managua: Meditations on Politics and Art*, a collection of newspaper articles I wrote after returning from a trip to Nicaragua and Costa Rica in 1989. To avoid repeating irresistible quotations from my favourite authors, I have pared back a few of the essays; and, in the interests of clarity and decency, I have removed some of my more embarrassing early pronouncements. For the most part, however, I have chosen to live with my enthusiasms and naivety. I owe much to the example of Robert Hass, whose *Twentieth-Century Pleasures* is a model from which any essayist or critic might learn in spades. John Berger's *And Our Faces, My Heart, Brief as Photos* stands, too, as a touchstone, a constant reminder that the best essays are able to hold their own alongside poetry. Against such high standards, my little book must stand as a failure, but it is a hard-won failure from whose deficiencies some small pleasure might yet be derived, some small lessons still be learned.

Gary Geddes, April 2009

. . . *we are responsible, nonetheless, for what we know and what we do not know, for the language we use and the language we accept from others, for the newspapers we read and the votes we cast, for the food and the books we buy, for the films we watch and the poems we read, to ourselves and to our children. And we are responsible for the choice: to be party to, or dissident. This is also a spiritual matter.*

John Burnside

1: A Perfect Reciprocity

In 1987, I had the opportunity to interview human rights workers and victims of the coup in Chile. The accounts of torture and disappearances at the hands of the military were devastating, but the courage in the bruised and weathered faces of those willing to risk their lives to bear witness was uplifting. One of the most inspiring witnesses was Jaime Hallas, publisher of the Chilean magazine *Análisis*. A tall bearded man, Hallas and his staff had been threatened with closure, torture and worse; in fact, his foreign affairs editor had been murdered by Pinochet's thugs. In response to my question about Chilean censorship, Hallas could not help smiling. "Here your books may survive," he said, stroking his thick beard, "but you may not." I thought of the Chilean musician Victor Jara lying dead in the stadium with his hands smashed for daring to stir the prisoners to song; I thought of Neruda, fleeing through the Cordilleras to Argentina years earlier as copies of his *Canto General* were clandestinely printed and distributed in Santiago; and I thought of Nain Nomez and Leandro Urbina, my Chilean friends, contemporary exiles from the terror, living and trying to write in Canada.

Back home I was able to ponder the fate of the writer and his book in Canada, where, as Margaret Atwood says, a writer can say anything he or she wants because no one is listening; or where, to quote Robertson Davies, being a writer "is as innocuous, as laudable without being in the least significant, as being a manufacturer of yoghurt." In Chile, where poets abound and where two Nobel Prizes have been won for poetry, our small group of Canadian visitors was given a stirring welcome and made to feel that the writing of poetry is one of the highest callings. Here, at best, our writers are subsidized into silence, since government funding and policy seem designed to make sure that the book is never found in school libraries or classrooms where it might radically alter the way in which we view society. So the writer, who might prove a potent force in his own times if driven to find other means to express his outrage at the status quo or his profound love for life-enriching social forms, is quietly co-opted with a small grant and the illusion of an audience for his slim volumes. Not much has really changed since A.M. Klein described the poet as "a number, an x, / a Mr Smith in a hotel register, — / incognito lost, lacunal."

Conventional wisdom has maintained the power of poetry to praise, mourn, and ridicule, to keep a record of the tribe, to induce trance, mobilize the troops, drive demons out of the psyche or body politic, and put men and women in touch with their deeper feelings. And yet criticism and journalism are still full of debate over the desirability of a link between poetry and politics. In his poem called "Politics," Yeats repudiates Thomas Mann's statement that we are all political animals and asserts the pre-eminence of the sensual world: "How can I, that girl standing there, / My attention fix / On Roman or on Russian / or on Spanish politics?" He starts with a rhetorical question and ends with this exclamation: "But O that I were young again / And held her in my arms!" In other words, skip the union meeting or environmental protest and spend the day in the sack.

I have no doubt about the power of the poetry as a verdict, a critique, and a spiritual call-to-arms, even in this debased, post-literate age. According to Palestinian writer Jabra I. Jabra, "As the sciences take over in the organization of society, the poet's intuition may not be heeded so much, but it remains operative at a certain level in the collective life where society finds nourishment, if not actual salvation, in its secret dreams. The poet thus remains an unexpected determinant of action, a motivator of change." Watch out when a poet puts the right words in the right order, insists American poet Robert Hass: "Because rhythm has direct access to the unconscious," he says, "because it can hypnotize us, enter our bodies and make us move, it has power. And power is political."

In W.H. Auden's elegy on the death of Yeats, there is a line that is often quoted by those who reject the notion that poetry has a political dimension, that it can be a vehicle for personal or social change. When the speaker of Auden's poem suggests that "poetry makes nothing happen," it's important to realize that he is uttering a sentiment Yeats would have endorsed, not stating his own philosophy. Auden makes his own very different position abundantly clear in his essays when he says:

In our age, the mere making of a work of art is itself a political act. So long as artists exist, making what they please and think they ought to make, even if it is not terribly good, even if it appeals only to a handful of people, they remind the Management of something managers need to be reminded of, namely, that the managed are a people with faces, not anonymous members, that *Homo Laborens* is also *Homo Ludens*.

American poet James Scully, in his book *Line Break: Poetry as Social Practice*, disputes the notion that political poetry is a contradiction in terms. In a chapter called "The Dream of An Apolitical Poetry," he writes: "Political poetry is not a contradiction in terms, but *an instructive redundancy*. It does not hold the mirror up to nature. It holds social reality up to the sheep, showing poetry its own face, its condition, its grounds and horizons. Showing, finally, that there is no poetry that is not political and that 'apolitical' and 'political' both have a political project—but one dreams transcendence, denial, immobility, whereas the other admits and treasures its problematical, restive, historical situation." (italics mine)

2

The situation for the poet in Canada is certainly problematical, restive, and steeped in history. The Canadian poet must write out of an awareness of institutionalized cultural duality that too often ignores the languages and social conditions of the first inhabitants and pays mere lip-service to a plurality of immigrant languages and cultures; he must write out of a federal-provincial dualism that encourages him, on the one hand, to explore a sense of place and local history while, on the other, pressuring him to articulate a national consciousness. And—god help the poor sod—he must write out of an acute consciousness of a political history that makes him both the guardian and celebrant of our difference from the United States and its remarkable homogenizing apparatus. Add to these concerns those of natives and feminists, who might well reject all of the above considerations as imperialist or patriarchal, and you have a recipe for silence or, at best, confusion.

It's not surprising, then, to find Northrop Frye pointing his finger in 1943 at "a certain abdication of political responsibility in our poetry. ... The Canadian poet likes to be objective ... he has a good seat on the revolutionary sidelines, and his poetic tendencies, reflective, observant, humorous, critical, and quite frankly traditional, show it." What's worse, Frye says, the Canadian poet also suffers from a sort of imaginative paralysis as a result of his colonial mentality:

> The colonial position of Canada is therefore a frostbite at the roots of the Canadian imagination, and it produces a disease for which I think the best name is prudery. By this I do not mean reticence in sexual matters: I mean the instinct to seek a conventional or commonplace expression of an idea. Prudery that keeps the orthodox poet from making a personal recreation of his orthodoxy: prudery that prevents the heretic from forming an articulate heresy that will shock: prudery that makes the radical stutter and gargle over all realities that are not physical: prudery that chokes off social criticism for fear some other group of Canadians will take advantage of it.

Frye's observations are certainly a provocative, if inaccurate, challenge to Canadian literature, which has shown signs of significant social and political awareness from the earliest times. More than a century ago, Alexander McLaughlin penned his famous proletarian verses that ridicule licking the hand that holds our noses to the wheel; and in 1899, Archibald Lampman created his nightmare vision of the technological future in "City At the End of Things." In this century Frank Scott wrote various satirical poems about Canadian politics and social policy; A.M. Klein paid the price for his insights into the depravities of Nazism and was rendered incapable of completing the great work of personal and collective healing started in *The Rocking Chair*; Dorothy Livesay published her documentary poem "Call My People Home," about the incarceration of Japanese-Canadians during World War II; Irving Layton unzipped his poetic bazooka for an assault on the Puritan mentality and the groves of academe; Earle Birney produced his verse drama, "The Damnation of Vancouver" and his poetic satires sending up attitudes in Anglo-Saxon Street, Toronto and in rural backwaters of Canada and the U.S., as well as his amazing travel poems about being a well-heeled and guilty gringo in Latin America.

This tradition continued unabated with a whole spate of playwrights and poets taking on the establishment and its historians: Carol Bolt's *Red Emma*, Sharon Pollock's *Komagata Maru*, George Ryga's *The Ecstasy of Rita Joe*, Tomson Highway's *Rez Sisters* on stage and Milton Acorn, Al Purdy, Pat Lowther, Tom Wayman, Bill Bissett, Lionel Kearns, Dennis Lee, Erin Mouré, and many others making guerrilla attacks from the foothills of Parnassus. And not all the targets were home-grown. On May 8, 1970, four days after the killings of students by the Ohio National Guard at Kent State, Al Purdy wrote "Picture Layout in *Life Magazine*," a powerful indictment of American values, which would place images of dead bodies in the Mekong Delta alongside consumer ads and high-society gossip: "On the homefront: / pretty cutout dresses in the next four pages / of the U.S. President's three little Nixon women / smiling about their new wardrobe / paper dolls for nice American children / to clip with blunt scissors / and paste over the bodies of the dead Vietnamese."

Not far over the horizon were such contemporary long poems and documentaries as "The Pride" by John Newlove, *The Clallam* by Frank Davey, and *Coppermine* by Don Gutteridge, each of which would play a signficant role in working out *a poetics of recall*, whereby the idiosyncrasies, failures, and shame of the tribe could be put permanently on display.

3

Reminding the management. Remembering is the means by which we survive individually and collectively, and recording or bearing witness is one of the chief functions of poetry. Most new regimes, whether Chilean or Chinese or Canadian, try to destroy the records or the recorders, sometimes both. As Welsh poet David Jones says in the Preface to *Anathemata*, poetry is

> a kind of *anamnesis* of, i.e. is an effective recalling of, something loved. In that sense it is inevitably 'propaganda', in that any real formal expression propagands the reality which caused those forms and their content to be. ... Insofar as poets call up the old order, or remind us of the ideal, they are dangerous to the state, to the new order. Thus they are suppressed or patronized accordingly.

To recreate a poetics of recall, Canadian poets first have to overcome certain false notions about the country, perpetrated by government, vested interests, and educational institutions committed to maintaining the status quo. The fact that Lester Pearson was awarded the Nobel Peace Prize for his Suez negotiations is often used to foster the notion that Canada is a natural peace-keeper, somehow morally superior and without crass or imperial ambitions, though nothing could be further from the truth. In these troubled times, when faith in political institutions and hope for a united country are at an all-time low, there is less pretence of innocence, less avoidance of troubling moments in our history, and less of a tendency to blame Canadian problems on external sources. This is nowhere more evident than in poetic responses to our ongoing political crisis, which Lord Durham once described as "two nations warring in the bosom of a single state".

In reaction to calls for Quebec independence in the late '70s, Al Purdy wrote a poem and tribute to René Lévesque called "A Handful of Earth," which begins with this surprising proposal: "let us join Quebec / if Quebec won't join us / I don't mind in the least / being governed from Quebec City / by *Canadiens* instead of Canadians / in fact the fleur-de-lis and maple leaf / in my bilingual guts / bloom incestuous."

Not very profound, you say, and a little sentimental? Well, notice how wonderfully textured the poem is in terms of sound and how it tries, nonetheless, to bring politics down to a personal level, to that sense of belonging that is so central to the issue of a linguistically secure Quebec and a united Canada. What follows is a very Canadian and Purdyesque catalogue of images and memories, where the same wind is shown to brush the tall firs on Vancouver Island as whispers along *Côte des Neiges* in Montreal, and where the poet recalls drinking coffee with a chain-smoking René Lévesque at *Parti Québécois* headquarters:

> I say to him now: my place is here
> whether Côte des Neiges Avenue Christophe Colombe
> Yonge Street Toronto Halifax or Vancouver
> this place is where I stand
> where all my mistakes were made
> when I grew awkwardly and knew what I was
> and that is Canadian or Canadien
> it doesn't matter which to me
>
> Sod huts break the prairie skyline
> then melt in rain
> the hip-roofed houses of New France as well
> but French no longer
> nor are we any longer English
> --limestone houses
> lean-tos and sheds our fathers built

in which our mothers died
before the forests tumbled down
ghost habitations
only this handful of earth
for a time at least
I have no other place to go

In an Afterword to *The Journals of Susanna Moodie*, Margaret Atwood once described the condition of violent duality in Canadian life as "paranoid schizophrenia." Her sequence of "Two-Headed Poems" is a biting and deadly humorous attempt to explore the national political crisis in terms of the problematic of two dominant cultures, to which she adds the threat of American take-over. Establishing the strategy of poet as satirist, stand-up comic, and *agent provocateur*, she examines various facets of our collective psyche in the poems—our endless political naivety, the possible illusion of our uniqueness from the U.S., the shock of recognizing how quickly we have adopted clichés and Madison Avenue slogans, the sense of disappointment in our elected leaders, and how the battle of the languages has perhaps betrayed us into losing sight of language itself as a precious resource to be celebrated and cultivated.

In one powerful section, she lays out, prophetically, the steps by which Canada and its richly diverse cultures will, as a result of blindness, internal bickering, and lack of vigilance, be swallowed up by outside forces, with everything "falling south / into the dark pit left by Cincinnati / after it crumbled." In the rubble of bumper-stickers, the stockpile of words and values, in a country "too small anyway / to be, as they say, viable."

The voice of the American in these poems, ugly as it is, sounds disturbingly like our own. Section V examines the bicultural war of words, where, ironically, bigotted unilingual rhetoric, whether Québécois or English-Canadian, destroys the very language it sets out to preserve, turning it all into political slogans. "We wanted to describe the snow ... in a language so precise / and secret ... there could be no translation"; instead, "Our hearts are flags now, / they wave at the end of each / machine we can stick them on."

Out of this moral and spiritual chaos emerges the ambiguous leader of the two-headed people of Canada, a Mr Shrug, Monsieur Comme Ci/Comme Ça, who turns out to be part chameleon, part bilingual Frankenstein. When I first read this poem, I was reminded of a comic-book Pierre Trudeau, then it seemed equally applicable to caricatures of Brian Mulroney, Paul Martin and Stephen Harper:

> Our leader
> is a man of water
> with a tinfoil skin.
>
> He has two voices,
> therefore two heads, four eyes,
> two sets of genitals, eight
> arms and legs and forty
> toes and fingers.
> Our leader is a spider,
>
> he traps words.
> They shrivel in his mouth,
> he leaves the skins.
>
> Most leaders speak
> for themselves, then
> for the people.
> Who does our leader speak for?
> How can you use two languages
> and mean what you say in both?

No wonder our leader scuttles
sideways, melts in hot weather,
corrodes in the sea, reflects
light like a mirror,
splits our faces, our wishes,
is bitter.

Our leader is a monster
sewn from dead soldiers,
a siamese twin.

Why should we complain?
He is ours and us,
we made him.

In the final section, the debate turns to questions
of linguistic dominance, here rendered in terms of
versions of the traditional French-English clichés,
prejudices, and put-downs that each of us resorts to
regarding the other language, which, like our own, is little
more than distasteful medicine, "a disease / of the mouth."
Instead of our dreams, to be mute or to achieve a language
"which rises liquid and effortless," Canadians find
themselves the keepers of "a duet / with two deaf singers."

Although written in a very public mode, this
sequence is neither doctrinaire nor programmatic. Each
poem makes its appeal through wit and playfulness,
rather than bombast or blatant sermonizing. Neither side
in the French-English debate is privileged; Atwood is even
scrupulous in balancing her anti-Americanism with biting
satire of Canadian attitudes. The poet establishes a series
of wildly ironic voices and proceeds to orchestrate her
vision through the use of black humour and bizarre
images of breakdown and decay, the falling movement of
the verse being perfectly in accord with the sinking state

of the nation, its slow and possibly inexorable descent into the bosom of the U.S.

Canadian poets have not all ignored the national crisis, though they are more often given to elegies than to diatribes, denunciations, or analysis. If the truth be told, we are a nation of mourners, from our own Oliver Goldsmith's "Elegy" to Lampman's gloomy and doomed "City at the End of Things," and to Dennis Lee's brilliant funereal pronouncements in *Civil Elegies*. The grandfather of contemporary despair over the future of Canada is, of course, the late George Grant, whose *Lament for A Nation* did much to galvanize nationalist feelings among Central Canadian writers of the '60s and '70s. Grant recognized that Canadian sovereignty had been sold in exchange for so-called technological progress and that both internationalism and ideological relativism were masks that needed to be denounced: "... if we skip the state of nationalism," Grant said, "we become not internationals (there are no such creatures) but Americans. It's as simple as that."

Grant did not live to witness the travesty of the Free Trade Agreement, which wiped out so many home-grown industries and set the country on a downward spiral in terms of equity and fair labour practices. Stephen Leacock, however, anticipated the pro-Canada spin with which our trade negotiators tried to fool us, when they intimated they'd snookered their US counterparts: "When an American tells you you've driven a hard bargain, you know he's taken you to the cleaners."

The debate about the future of Canada, or *duet with two deaf singers*, is only one of many issues confronting the Canadian poet in a troubled world, but it is surely one of the more pressing. E.J. Pratt, in a very different climate, was able to present the building of the national railway in comic opera, or mock-epic, terms, events fueled by Scottish oatmeal, triumphant technology, and a certain alcoholic political wizardry, in which the threat of American take-over is rendered in terms of nothing more serious than courtship rituals. The French-English duality scarcely figures in his narrative. Times have changed. Frank Scott took Pratt to task for ignoring the exploited Chinese coolies; writers today, such as John Newlove, might well question Pratt's *Towards the Last Spike* for ignoring the displacement of Native peoples, over whose lands the steel road snaked.

The Western Canadian poet is more likely to find inspiration in region, or place, than in national or pan-Canadian concerns; he is also more likely to draw political significance from the aboriginal contract—or absence of one—than from French-English or Canadian-American dualities. The re-emergence of such regional and aboriginal concerns has greatly complicated present constitutional negotiations, especially where provincial governments have not been anxious to be locked into the settlement of land claims and the acknowledgement of aborginal rights. How we connect with our aboriginal heritage is the subject of John Newlove's long poem "The Pride."

Newlove poses a question that will always be central to Canadian life and to our ongoing constitutional wrangling: "the knowledge of / our origins, and where / we are in truth, / whose land this is / and is to be." In his middle and later poems, particularly "The Pride" and "Crazy Riel", Newlove moves away from the song of the dispossessed self to explore the grief of the tribe, focussing on the destruction of aboriginal peoples. After calling up images of the Pawnee and Sioux, destroyed by white racism and greed, Newlove begins a roll-call of the ghosts of Raven, d'Sonoqua, and the great Indian leaders of the Plains: "they are all ready / to be found, the legends / and the people, or / all their ghosts and memories, / whatever is strong enough / to be remembered."

Here, the poet is cultural anthropologist, or archaeologist, digging up the vanishing fragments, shaping them, rendering them in terms of art, finding the "roots / and rooted words", "the pride, the grand poem / of our land, of the earth itself", making these memories strong enough to resist erasure: "a single line / and then the sunlit brilliant image suddenly floods us / with understanding, shocks our / attentions, and all desire / stops."

Now, native and non-native Canadians alike are suddenly called upon to address the ongoing rape and degradation of the planet, which sees wetlands being destroyed, old growth forests clear-cut, fish stocks and habitats ruined, air and water supplies privatized, polluted. Poetry must address these losses, resist these forces and, most of all, praise the creatures of the earth, while they last. I shall let the vagueness of the pronoun "they" stand to link the poet with other endangered species.

4

I want to conclude by stressing that, if the writing of poetry is a subversive activity, then its power to subvert has as much to do with formal considerations as with the choice of subject matter. To make these moments of our history *strong enough to be remembered*, the poet needs all the resources of language at his disposal, just as he needs to put all his own psychic and intellectual resources at the disposal of the language, in a perfect reciprocity. Some of our poets are less overtly political, choosing the less obvious but equally significant task of sharpening the language, or being themselves sharpened by listening to the language. That, too, is a political act of great importance. As Denise Levertov suggests:

...it is the poet who has language in his care; the poet who more than others recognizes language as a form of life and a common resource to be cherished and served as we should serve and cherish earth and its waters, animal and vegetable life, and each other. The would-be poet who looks on language merely as something to be used, as the bad farmer or the rapacious industrialist looks on the soil or on rivers merely as things to be used, will not discover a deep poetry; he will only, according to the degree of his skill, construct a counterfeit or less acceptable—a subpoetry, at best efficiently representative of his thought or feeling—a reference, not an incarnation. And he will be contributing, even if not in any immediately apparent way, to the erosion of language, just as the irresponsible, irreverent farmer and industrialist erode the land and pollute the rivers.

The Canadian political reality appears as troubled as ever, though, in my view, it is showing signs of health in its continuing self-analysis and susceptibility to change. I agree with B. C. playwright and political scientist Herschel Hardin when he observes that

It is because Canadian civilization is so vulnerable, because every once in a while it seems to be coming apart at the seams under the pressure of centrifugal forces, that it has been so fruitful, and has slowly developed a subterranean strength. Nothing has added to that strength, and to that vulnerability, more than the separatist movement, and English Canada's facing up to the possibility it symbolizes.

To Hardin's statement, we must add John Newlove's words about knowing our origins; and we must be vigilant and persistent in land claims negotiations, redress and the settlement of disputes, reminders of the centrality of the aboriginal fact in our national life.

General Pinochet gave up power in no small measure thanks to the poets and musicians and intellectuals who resisted and spoke out against his tyranny. The list of his abuses and atrocities, many of them placed permanently on record by Chilean writers and by some of our own poets, condemn him in history. Canadian politicians should ponder this fact when they play fast and loose with national symbols such as Via Rail, Canada Post, the National Film Board, CBC and Canada Council for the Arts, and when they endorse agreements, commercial and industrial take-overs and massive projects that threaten our sovereignty, social programs, natural resources, particularly water, and environment. Poets will continue to name the names and commit them to the public memory.

Brazilian theorist Paolo Freire once said,

To exist, humanly, is to name the world, to change it. Once named, the world in its turn reappears to the namers as a problem and requires of them a new naming ... . There is no true word that is not at the same time a praxis. Thus, to speak a true word is to transform the world.

Like Chile, which has undergone so profound a trauma, Canada is struggling to give itself a new name and a new definition, one that, I hope, will be capable of constant adaptation to this rapidly changing world.

I come back to the comment of Chilean publisher Jaime Hallas: *your books may survive, but you may not.* So be it. None of us will survive, except in those words and works that help our peoples remember—and dream.

And that, in general, is our task.

Sources:

George Grant, *Lament for a Nation*; Northrop Frye, *The Bush Garden*; Paolo Freire, *Pedagogy of the Oppressed*; W.H. Auden, *The Dyer's Hand*; Gary Geddes (ed.), *Divided We Stand*; Herschel Hardin, *A Nation Unaware*; Denise Levertov, *The Poet in the World: New and Selected Essays*.

2: Country Music

When I was a small boy weeding a two-acre potato patch in Saskatchewan, I used to sing at the top of my lungs all the latest country-western songs on the radio, before I realized it was politically incorrect for a Canadian to do so. My favourite was a tear-jerker about a drunkard's son in the attic of a dusty old tenement, who was beaten regularly and took solace in crying for his dead mother. Although the source is American, it's not a bad image for Canadians, inhabiting the attic of North America, offspring of a drunken nation-building prime minister and two absentee mothers, England and France, who, if not dead, are embalmed and in permanent exile. We have the dust, too, and the clear sense that we don't really own the land we inhabit; morally, it belongs to the Indians, but, in fact, it's mostly controlled by foreign investors. And we take an inverse pride in the regular beatings we endure, economically and culturally, at the hands of our ungainly neighbour to the south.

Later, as a young subaltern in the Royal Canadian Navy, I sailed out among the icebergs from Halifax harbour on Canada's east coast, to the sounds of country western music. You can't escape country western music anywhere in Canada, especially in the east; ask Hank Snow. So it's not surprising to find Bronwen Wallace, one of our best poets, writing a tribute to country singer Emmylou Harris, *Keep That Candle Burning Bright*. In her dedication, Wallace speaks of her own frustrated desire to be a real-live singer, not just a poet, and of being forced too often to be content with "mouthing the words" (10). What she has to say about this genre is fascinating for several reasons, not the least of which is the poignantly implicit notion that she listens not only to that music on behalf of several disenfranchised sub-groups—the poor, the homeless, and the deserted, obviously—but also on behalf of women, poets in particular, and Canadians in general.

Wallace celebrates what is "homely" about the genre, "the way it sings on, using its breaking to do it." (18) Implicit here is the idea of Wallace's life and poetry itself as a "hurtin" song. And Canada, too, as the great narrative of betrayal, treachery, and impending divorce. Wallace quickly draws the parallels between her prose and poetic narratives and the parables of the music genre: "I'm always amazed at what we tell", she says, "how much faith we put in it. Never really knowing who is listening, how they're going to take it" (21). That's part of being a Canadian, too, trying to imagine who's listening. Morley Callaghan once thought only Americans were listening, so he changed the setting of his stories to please his perceived audience.

In a section called "Cowboy Angel", Wallace describes how the song always reminds her of a man she met and fell in love with on the transcontinental train in winter, heading through the mountains from Edmonton to Vancouver:

We flew straight across that rivered bridge last night, half-past two is how the song puts it. How remembering, like dreaming, is a way of driving all night, billboards and truck-stops flashing past with the voices on the radio, the miles bringing them in and letting them out into the smell of rain, the crying of a train whistle somewhere. Somewhere out there. Where the last arc of a conductor's flashlight rounds us and flows on over the other passengers, their dark, rich breathing filling the curves and hollows of their sleep, until the sun comes up, bringing the mountains with it, the wait in the thick, hot smoke from the breaks, his cigarettes, our kisses, my cowboy angel stepping off into clouds that carry him away as the train starts up again, light rushing out over rocks and the branches of trees, snow flying faster and faster no matter how fast I go.

While country music, for all its emotional shallows and clichés, touches something deep in Canadian and American psyches, I want to use the term in a broader sense, to speak of the kinds of word-music a country produces to articulate its urge not just to survive, but also to grow—is it too much to hope?—in grace. The metaphor Wallace gives us of train travel is not a bad place to start either, since the building of the railway, rather than, say, a civil war, was the principal activity that would guarantee the establishing of a nation from sea to sea. The transcontinental railway served as a major symbol of national unity for more than a century, during the latter years of which the Canadian Broadcasting Corporation began to lay down its own invisible tracks of national sound on the airwaves.

Since a great deal of drama and magic attaches to the building and operating of the railway, it's hardly surprising that two of our major poets, E.J. Pratt and bpNichol, should have chosen the railway as subject and the long poem as vehicle. Pratt's *Towards the Last Spike* (1952), written about the drama and machinations of building the railway, and Nichol's *Continental Trance* (1982), written as a journey into self and language at the very moment the railway was being abandoned by government as a subsidized mode for transporting people, were published exactly thirty years apart.

2

Towards the Last Spike is written in the mock-epic tradition, so it begins tongue-in-cheek, determined to have fun with its sources, which it does promptly with an epic simile on the effects of oatmeal on the predominantly Scottish builders and financiers of the line:

> Oatmeal was in their blood and in their names.
> Thrift was the title of their catechism.
> It governed all things but their mess of porridge
> Which, when it struck the hydrochloric acid
> With treacle and skim-milk, became a mash.
> Entering the duodenum, it broke up
> Into amino acids: then the liver
> Took on its natural job as carpenter:
> Foreheads grew into cliffs, jaws into juts.
> The meal, so changed, engaged the follicles:
> Eyebrows came out as gorse, the beards as thistles,
> And chest-hair the fell of Grampian rams.
> It stretched and vulcanized the human span:
> Nonagenarians worked and thrived upon it.
> Out of such chemistry its fearsome racial products:—
> The power to strike a bargain like a foe,
> To win an argument upon a bury,
> Invest the language with a Bannockburn,
> Culloden or the warnings of Lochiel. ...

It's a writerly long poem, preoccupied with language, speech, accent, metaphor, tongues, words in general, and, as the previous quotation suggests, rhetoric or *argument*. Pratt's narrator describes the building of the transcontinental railway as "the battle of ideas and words / And kindred images called by the same name." In this regard the poem recalls Howard O'Hagan's *Tay John* published thirteen years earlier, also about the building of a railway, a novel whose second section "Hearsay," begins:

"In the year 1904, and in the years that followed, a new name blew up against the mountains and an idea stirred like a wind through the valleys." The word O'Hagan's narrator is referring to is "progress."

Both writers share an awareness of the power of words and ideas, but the earlier period Pratt dramatizes is characterized less by certainty than by yearnings that resist articulation. In fact, *Towards the Last Spike* begins with the idea of Canada not as fact, but as a speech impediment, a stutter, a mere verbal potential. The unutterable ambitions, compounded of ambition, greed, yearning for power, and the fear of American imperialism, result in a colossal, ongoing argument, which pretty well sums up our idea of Canada even today, where everything is a text waiting to be revised, quoted out of context, in which even the triangular mountains seem to possess a "prose severity".

The battle of words is fought, primarily, by our alcoholic Prime Minister, the Tory leader John A. Macdonald, who combines whisky with oatmeal to fuel his speech and replenish his word-hoard. He coins "From sea to sea", which he considers "a hallowed phrase," and falls asleep toying with that "Most excellent word. . . pioneers!" to describe the conceivers and builders of the line. He has to keep on his toes to win the hand of The Lady of British Columbia, in order to outsmart that smooth, fast-talking Latino-lover, California. But his chief adversary is language itself in the form of a member of the Liberal opposition, Edward Blake, who, like his partial namesake, has an unfortunate gift for spinning powerful metaphors.

Blake, who draws nutrition from parliamentary recesses as if they are sandwiches and turns that energy into words, brings down the government with his oratory: "Each word, each phrase, each clause went to position, / Each sentence regimented like a lockstep." Pratt recognizes the essential ingredients of political debate—rhetoric and show business—evident even in how the word "pass" (as in Yellowhead Pass) is pronounced:

> The leaders of the factions in the House
> And through the country spelled the word the same:
> The way they got their tongue around the word
> Was different, for some could make it hiss
> With sound of blizzards screaming over ramparts ...

Blake's eloquence reaches its height when he describes the railway project as an attempt "*To build a Road over that sea of sterile mountains.*"

Macdonald is reduced to praying, "God send us no more metaphors / Like that—except from Tory factories." When the work proceeds, ordinary workers band together, surrendering their identity in the great project of nation-building, but acquiring thereby the "gift of tongues" to give new settlements, as yet scarcely more than acts of faith, a name. The land is there to be read, much as Magellan did when he "tried to read / The barbarous language of his Strait": the lizard shield with its bottomless (one might almost say unfathomable) logic and bogs; and the mountains, so resistant to interpretation, where "The men bored in, / The mesozoic rock arguing the inches." Macdonald, known by the oxymoron Old Tomorrow, finally runs out of argument and stories, the bullshit factor; however, whisky and money save the day and the line is completed.

Pratt has not exactly written a critique of early or late capitalism—or even a challenge to existing ideologies.

He celebrates financiers, the two Donalds (Smith and Stephen), for risking their personal fortunes in the venture; he also celebrates the indomitableness of Van Horne, who oversaw most of the construction. Frank Scott has asked where the Chinese coolies who had built the railway are in Pratt's mock-epic; we might also ask where individual workers are, not to mention the French-Canadians and First Nations. The doomed Métis leader Louis Riel and the full-breeds, as Pratt calls them, appear briefly, but only as possible obstacles in the grand scheme, less significant by far than bogs, mountains, or cash shortages.

However, *Towards the Last Spike* is anything but a simple paean to mindless nation-building and cant about progress. The last spike is never far from being the last straw. The poem begins with the idea of a larger Canada as a speech impediment, a stutter, proceeds to parody the public and parliamentary debate surrounding the construction of a transcontinental railway, and ends not only with a bent spike at the driving-in ceremony, but also with Van Horne unable to articulate his feelings, spitting out "some phlegm / To ratify the tumult with 'Well Done' / Tied in a knot of monosyllables."

3

bpNichol begins his long poem *Continental Trance* with a pun that reverses the word order in his title and thus shifts attention from the railway as product to the trip by rail as process. He also begins in Vancouver and heads east, as if running the film of Pratt's narrative in reverse, not inappropriately, since the headlines in the papers as he leaves the west coast announce: "GOVERNMENT AXES

TRANS-CONTINENTAL LINE THRU JASPER". The poem promptly parodies its literary origins with a passage of epic erasure:

> minus the ALL ABOARD
>
> minus my father waving
>
> minus the CN logo
>
> minus my mother waving
>
> minus seventeen years of my life
> Ellie & me
> our unborn child in her belly
> heading east
> out of Vancouver
> July 27th
> 8 p.m.
> nineteen eighty-
> 1.

Nichol dispenses with causality and the idea of the poem as pure aesthetic object, using the pun "train of thot" and proposing language as principal vehicle, welcoming readers "aboard this mixed metaphor," "this paradox."

Privileging the activity of chance, or randomness, seems central to his poem, where rhyme or song "keeps butting in", and where passing objects serve as unexpected but useful means of tripping the linguistic switches. Early in the poem Nichol admits that "random information intrudes each time I ride these rails;" later, this fact is offered as poetics:

> so there it is
>
> the literal metaphor or symbol
>
> linear narrative of random sequential thots

accidents of geography, history & circumstance

the given

What we have, instead of the building of the railway, is the construction of tracks of language, not just the poetic main-line, but trunk-lines, branch-lines of meaning, drawn from a playful mind using associative logic: "notation / in the landscape of a nation & / a revelation."

If the reference to nation and revelation in a postmodern epic of this sort seems surprising, it might be useful to be reminded that Nichol's poetic project throughout the *Martyrology* has been essentially religious and political, in the sense that his mysticism, like William Blake's, has profound implications for the structures of self and society.

"Where is this poem going?"
"Toronto"

"What does it teach us?"
"how coincidence reaches into our lives
and instructs us"

the 19th century knew
any narrative, like life,
is where coincidence leads you

Unlike some of his contemporaries, Nichol does not struggle against the idea of narrative. While he may be unravelling and deconstructing *Towards the Last Spike*, he is quite conscious of Pratt's own linguistic playfulness; no doubt that's why he chose "st utter" as one of his two principal verbal saints here, since the reference takes us deliberately back to the stutter at the beginning of Pratt's long poem. The second one, "st ate", is equally significant, since, like Pratt, Nichol seems to be saying that all human action, whether building a railway, a poem, a life, or a nation is first and foremost a linguistic operation, a state of mind.

The idea of a nation in parenthesis, like the concept of self, as something that will vanish, that holds in its inception the seeds of its own undoing and disappearance, is central to *Continental Trance*. Nichol contemplates his own death, remembers the death of his first child, and sees, perhaps, the axing of the railway as the beginning of the death of the idea of Canada. However, while the long poem, like the train, is "reaching for conclusions", Nichol wants to resist closure, just as he tries to resist the confines of self. He recalls the origins of the epic in the oral tradition, not as private property, but as belonging to "a community of speakers". In the final sections of his poem he not only gives a nod to both baseball and to the epic tradition with his pun "a finality Homer", but also recalls, or recovers, Plato's allegory of the cave, which postulates the world we know as a world of shadows. Ironically, the image of Plato is not imposed on the poem from without, but introduced by chance from dwelling on the preceding image of the sky *caving in*.

In other words, by listening to the unfolding wordscape of the poem, and being attentive to our passage through humanscapes and landscapes, we learn where to go, running on tracks we no longer perceive." Nichol's poem, unlike Pratt's, is intensely personal, yet it moves beyond the self by reading signs: "O-T-H-I-N-G", which he first takes to be the word "NOTHING" with one letter missing, turns out to have been "CLOTHING", prompting Nichol to confess: "like my life-long wish / that i might clothe myself finally in belief." As poem and train

slip into Toronto, sceptic, mystic, small-n nationalist
Nichol reads another sign offered up to him at random:

> scrawled across the one wall
> I WANTED TO BE AN ANARCHIST
>
> an ending
> in itself
> unending

4

Country music, to be sure, is found everywhere in
Canadian long and short poems. The lonely figure in A.
M. Klein's "Portrait of the Poet as Landscape" takes "a
green inventory / In world but scarcely uttered" (perhaps
he should have said "stuttered"); and Frank Scott, another
poet fascinated with the Canadian shield (a shield to
silence any of those dreamed by Homer) speaks of a place
"Inarticulate, artic" that must "choose its language." Scott's
italicized early image of "*A language of flesh and roses,*"
which will presumably come if we let technology lead,
seems naive and sadly ironic from our perspective of
having inherited a severely damaged eco-system; yet the
relation of language to technique gains in complexity as
the poem progresses:

> Now there are pre-words,
> Cabin syllables,
> Nouns of settlement
> Slowly forming, with steel syntax,
> The long sentence of its exploitation.

It's impossible to imagine any lawyer, never mind one of
Scott's reputation, using the word "sentence"

unselfconsciously, so the line must be acknowledged to carry considerable irony. However, in the final stanza of "Laurentian Shield", he predicts a deeper, more humane note, a new language, "written in the full culture of occupation."

Of course, the word "occupation" is itself highly charged with political significance; in fact, it's central to the debate Québécois are having about their future within the Canadian federation. They have felt themselves living in occupied territory, rendered almost invisible, to such an extent that they sometimes fail to see themselves occupiers of aboriginal land. And the whole country assumes, these days, a siege mentality as British and American right-wing agendas come to dominate, threatening to dismantle not only the railways and communications systems that bind us together, but also the hard-won network of social services.

Dennis Lee's *Civil Elegies* provided for the '60s an extended lament over the possible/inevitable demise of Canada under the pressure of what George Grant has called the American liberal-technological vision. Robert Kroetsch, in *Seed Catalogue*, working outside the tradition of pan-Canadian culture poems, has tried to champion the regional, the local, asking how we might grow a poet, how we might grow a prairie town. The answer, he suggests, is in developing the process of memory: struggling against cultural amnesia, writing about, and against, our own disappearance, as individuals, and as a people, or peoples. He presents us as gardeners, working to produce those hardier grains, winter wheats, that will survive any kind of weather; as lovers who, given all the inhibitions and prohibitions of life in a Puritan environment, can only survive by becoming subversive, or "playing dirty"; and as builders, taking our cues from gopher and groundhog, creating an underground culture that is not so easy to destroy.

Not surprisingly, Kroetsch too, in thinking about the task of the writer, is reminded of the railway, that great, if dubious and desperate, symbol of national unity. He quotes friend and novelist Rudy Wiebe, who takes the railway as his working metaphor: "You must lay great black steel lines of fiction, break up that space with huge design and, like the fiction of the Russian steppes, build a giant artifact. No song can do that." Kroetsch, of course, is too much a poet and postmodernist to accept at face-value Wiebe's totalizing vision. Highlighting the local, finding authenticity in the apparently trivial and random details of the ordinary life, Kroetsch proves that song, poetic song, is perhaps even better equipped to lay claim to that space.

The home place in *Seed Catalogue* is, ironically, a double hook that ties us to the land, *notre petit coin de la création*, but also forces us out again into the world, as if to say, we cannot love the world, in general, unless we first love one small piece of it in particular. Close to the end of this amazing long poem, Kroetsch subtly presents the conundrum:

(b)

No. 2362 — *Imperialis Morn-ing Glory:* "This is the wond-derful *Japanese Morning Glo-ry*, celebrated the world over for its *wondrous beauty* of both flowers and foliage."

Sunday, January 12, 1975. This evening after
rereading *The Double Hook:* looking at Japanese prints.
Not at actors. Not at courtesans. Rather: Hiroshige's
series, *Fifty-Three Stations on the Tokaido.*

From the *Tokaido* series: "Shono-Haku-u." The
bare-assed travellers, caught in a sudden shower,
men and trees, bending. How it is in a rain shower /
that you didn't see coming. And couldn't have avoided /
even if you had.

> The double hook:
> the home place.
> The stations of the way:
> the other garden
>
> *Flourishes.*
> *Under absolute neglect.*

Neither *Seed Catalogue* nor the two long poems I
have discussed in greater detail, are political manifestos,
but they have much to say about how we conduct
ourselves as a nation. If "absolute neglect" sounds too
much like *laissez-faire,* and an invitation to imperialists
other than morning glories, the level of tolerance and
benign neglect we want to cultivate as a national strategy
is still preferable to the rigidities of the unitary state. That
is the language, the country music, we are trying to
invent—this nation of saints and cowboys, angels and
alcoholics—stuttering, bare-assed, inarticulate, occupied
and preoccupied as we are with insurmountable egos,
moral quagmires, and conflicting agendas.

Sources

I am quoting here from Bronwen Wallace's *Keep That
Candle Burning Bright and Other Poems* (1991), E.J. Pratt's

Towards the Last Spike (1952), bpNichol's *Continental Trance* (1982), and Herschel Hardin's *A Nation Unaware* (1974).

3: The Long Poem as Potlatch: Going the Distance

1.

When Apollonius of Rhodes wrote the *Argonautica* in 5,834 lines, his friend Callimachus is said to have remarked that a long book is a great evil. I don't know what his observation did to their friendship, but I do know, judging from the low status long poems enjoy today, that Callimachus's sentiment would find plenty of support among poets and critics.

I might as well confess at the outset that, like Apollonius, I prefer a great evil in poetry to a minor good. Sometimes the literary sprinter strikes me as an aberration; the intense white heat at which he burns must finally consume him. But the long-distance poet burns long and gives heart far into the night; his art and his endurance bring to mind that great distance runner, Geoffrey Chaucer, who spoke of poetry as "the craft so long to lerne."

I don't want to run this metaphor into the ground, or divide the poetic world into hares and tortoises, with the critics placing all their bets on the flashy, hyper-kinetic leapers who are doomed to pass out by the roadside, while the stodgy, persistent plodders trudge weak-eyed and earnest towards the finish line. The scenario isn't that far-fetched, but we need all kinds of poets, the long-winded and those whose breath comes in short pants. What I want to do is make a case here for the long poem, in all its manifestations, as a form not only worthy of serious attention by poets, critics and anthologists, but also as a form peculiarly suited to our age.

There's no shortage of long poems around. A host of names comes readily to mind: Crane, Eliot, Williams, David Jones, Dorn, Neruda, MacDiarmid, Kunene, Birney, Berryman, Lowell, Atwood, McGrath, Ondaatje, Livesay, Dudek and Gutteridge, to name only a few. Yet, despite this abundance, little attention has been given to the study of the contemporary long poem or narrative. If one thinks of poetry in terms of its reductive and expansive extremes, it becomes perfectly obvious that the reductive impulse predominates in this century: the single image, the epigram, the final death-bed couplet that will put the lid on, once and for all, clearly hold more sway in the critics' minds than does a rousing narrative or a vast, sprawling epic. Could it be that there's something faintly indecent and embarrassing about the long poem, as if it couldn't quite get its act together, as if the poet had lost his eraser or run out of correcting fluid. The long poem—let's face it—reeks of impurity and excess.

Much of the blame for this attitude belongs on the shoulders of Edgar Allan Poe, a short story writer in poet's clothing. Poe claimed in 1848, in a lecture entitled "The Poetic Principle," that "a long poem does not exist. I maintain that the phrase 'a long poem' is a contradiction in terms." Poe argues that it is impossible to sustain the "elevating" effects of true poetry to any great length; after a time the poem lapses and ceases to be poetry. Thus he calls Milton's *Paradise Lost* not a unified whole, but a "series of minor poems" strung together; *The Iliad*, he says, is constructed on "an imperfect sense of art." Poe goes on to prophesy that "no very long poem will ever be popular again," insisting that value in poetry has nothing to do with "sustained effort" and that a work of art should be praised for the impression it makes rather than for its bulk. "The fact is," Poe concludes, "perseverance is one thing and genius quite another."

No one wants to argue for quantity over quality. However, Poe's anal-retentive theory of poetry deserves special recognition, perhaps a chair at Upper Rubber Boot College which we could call the Poe Chair. Poe was essentially a prose writer with his hand in the poetic till, robbing poetry for the sake of his own vested interests in another form. He loved narrative; his problem was that he did not know how to make narrative work within the bounds of his own narrow conception of poetry. His theories of composition did wonders for the short story, but nothing for the future of poetry.

Poe had obviously read Longinus on the sublime in art, where the view is expressed that "when a work is long, sleep eventually creeps over it." Poe was not alone in preferring the lyric. Coleridge, as David Lodge reminds us in *The Language of Fiction*, distinguished between lyric and "mere narrative," where "the style should be simpler."

For poets such as Valéry and Mallarmé, narrative was like walking, a destination always in view, while the lyric was akin to dance, an end in itself. Such purist analogies distort the issue. Poe's prescriptive criteria may have provided a useful counterbalance or antidote to the discursive and didactic excesses of his age, but they also lent themselves too readily to the emasculating or neutering of poetry as a vital, all encompassing literary form—one which has every bit as much power as the novel or drama to move audiences, to transmit important cultural information, to analyze the human condition, to exploit and preserve the dialect of the tribe, and to provide some much-needed entertainment along the way.

Poe no doubt anticipated the temper of the Modern period in painting, sculpture and literature, which is so well expressed in Ezra Pound's "A Retrospect" in 1917:

As to the twentieth-century poet, and poetry which I expect to see written during the next decade or so, it will, I think, move against poppy-cock, it will be harder and saner, it will be what Mr. Hewitt calls 'nearer the bone.' It will be as much like granite as it can be, its force will lie in its truth, its interpretive power (of course, poetic force does always rest there); I mean it will not try to seem forcible by rhetorical din, and luxurious riot. We will have fewer painted adjectives, impeding the shock and stroke of it. At least for myself, I want it so, austere, direct, free from emotional slither.

Out of these reductive extremes has come a wonderful clarity and precision, a new focus on the image and its power to evoke and recall; a healthy suspicion of adjectives and their power to blur our perceptions if used carelessly or in excess; and a concentration on verbs and nouns to provide movement and concreteness in a poem. The Imagist Movement produced some remarkable short poems; but its most important legacy consists in having provided a built-in editor—and a rather demanding one at that—for the century. The radical diminution of poetry that Pound spearheaded finds an echo in the words of British novelist B.S. Johnson, who dismisses narrative poets as "literary flat-earthers": "Poetry did not die when story-telling moved on. It concentrated on things it was still best able to do—the short, economical lyric, the intense emotional statement, depth rather than scale, exploitation of rhythms which made their optimum impact at short lengths but which would have become monotonous and unreadable if maintained longer than a few pages." The patronizing tone, it seems, goes with the turf.

An enormous price has been paid for this blinkered vision of poetry. The Imagists and, to a lesser extent, the Symbolists, as a result of the reductive extremes to which they went, may have rendered poetry of interest to an increasingly smaller audience. Here's what American poet Robinson Jeffers thought about the 'new poetics' as he walked through the countryside and pondered his future:

> But now, as I smelled the wild honey midway the trestle and meditated on the direction of modern poetry, my discouragement blackened. It seemed to me that Mallarmé and his followers, renouncing intelligibility in order to concentrate the music of poetry, had turned off the road into a narrowing lane. Their successors could only make further renunciations; ideas had gone, now meter had gone, imagery would have to go; then recognizable emotions would have to go; perhaps at last even words might have to go or give up their meaning, nothing be left but musical syllables. Every advance required the elimination of some aspect of reality, and what could it profit me to know the direction of modern poetry if I did not like the direction? It was too much like putting out your eyes to cultivate the sense of hearing, or cutting off the right hand to develop the left. These austerities were not for me; originality by amputation was too painful for me.

Poetry was once a feast for the ear, eye and the mind; it was a source of story, character, history, ideas, anything from the sacking of cities to the seduction of innocence, from divine thoughts to obscene gestures. The subjectivity and minimalism that characterizes so much of twentieth-century poetry is no longer acceptable. There's no reason for the poet to be content with a verbal snapshot, when he or she can aim for a verbal approximation of the wondrous sweep and illusion of the motion picture or the range and intensity of the symphony. It's time we stopped perpetrating the notion that poetry must be reduced to its bare essentials (or inessentials), which may be no more than a few faint scratches on the page and a few adjustments of the typewriter carriage as proof of life.

I am reminded of a comment by French novelist Patrick Grainville whose novel *Les Flamboyants*, though turned down as excessive by the literary publisher Gallimard, went on to win the Prix Goncourt. Asked what he was trying to achieve in this novel, which defied convention and whose shirttails were hanging out, Grainville replied:

A baroque adventure novel, flambouyant, superbaroque. I'm not afraid of bad taste. It emanates a kind of jubilation, surprise and delight in style you don't get from good taste. Sometimes I look at my excesses and I say to myself, why not? Literature is made from gifts, not refusals.

Poetry, too, is made from gifts, not refusals. Its existence in the life of our society depends upon its ability to absorb and assimilate new materials (linguistic and otherwise), to take upon itself the widest possible range of information, idea, event, theme. Technically, the poet cannot afford to give up any of the resources at his or her disposal. As D.G. James has said, "the imagination of the great poet at least never rests from this momentous labour which endeavours to encompass the whole of life, and to achieve a comprehensive unity of imaginative pattern." Earle Birney once described the long poems of E.J. Pratt as a "grand binge," rather than a starvation diet; and Roland Barthes once compared the poetic process with the potlatch. I am grateful that postmodernism seems to have moved from famine to feast.

Ezra Pound found himself boxed in by Imagism and soon abandoned it for wider, and greener, pastures. Writing in defence of Pound's long poems, particularly the *Cantos*, Scottish poet Hugh MacDiarmid claimed not only that Pound's primary poetic impulse was expansive, but also that Pound knew enough about life and about art to be both singer *and* sage. The three qualities he attributed to Pound were (1) robustness of thought, (2) felicity of expression, and (3) comprehensiveness of point of view. In an age of unprecedented change such as our own, MacDiarmid says, we can only rejoice in a poet who still has the power of synthesis. In Pound, he concludes, "stress is laid on the fact that we are living in a great quantitative rather than a qualitative age and that the only form adequate to the classless society is the epic—not like epics of the past, except in scale, but embodying a knowledge of the modern world and all its possibilities, not in bits and pieces, but in the round."

I believe that the long poem is not only fundamental to our age, but also that it is the fundamental proving ground for the poet. After a while the mature poet longs for a larger canvas, for which he needn't have recourse to prose or drama. This ought to come as a breath of fresh air to poets and readers who feel that poetry has become too minimal, or that critics are waxing more and more eloquent about less and less. (Is there a link between the tremendous growth of criticism and the near-demise of poetry as a form of arcana?) Some years ago, Northrop Frye expressed the hope that poets would "maintain an interest in narrative form. For the lyric, if cultivated too exclusively, tends to become too entangled with the printed page; in an age when new contacts between a poet and his public are opening up through radio, the narrative, a form peculiarly adapted for public reading, may play an important role in re-awakening a public respect for and response to poetry." Add to this the fact of television, an explosion in audio-visual media, internet, and government-sponsored readings, and you can see that conditions are certainly favourable for lifting poetry from its second-class status and from the obscurity of the printed page into the public arena.

T.S. Eliot has gone as far as anyone in replying, by way of both practice and precept, to Poe's theory that a long poem must inevitably bog down in its own juices. In his essay on the music of poetry, he says that

[...] in a poem of any length, there must be transitions between passages of less intensity, to give a rhythm of fluctuating emotion essential to the musical structure of the whole; and the passages of less intensity will be, in relation to the level on which the total poem operates, prosaic—so that, in the sense implied by that context, it may be said that no poet can write a poem of amplitude unless he is a master of the prosaic.

Even William Carlos Williams, who led a renewed attack on the narrative poem in the last century, found that he could not resist the lure of the long poem. In the Prologue to *Kora in Hell*, he insisted that "the world of action is a world of stones," that "nothing can be imparted by action." He succumbed, finally, to the long poem, with its narrative fragments, its images, ideas and documents. The expansive impulse reclaimed him, after a brief period as an imagist, because he had fallen in love with history and with place, two subjects that do not always lend themselves readily to the lyric, the image and the epigram. He needed a much larger canvas on which to explore the multifaceted character and history of Paterson, New Jersey, so he began to experiment with a special kind of brokenness of form that would be consistent with the non-rational, non-linear nature of experience as he saw it. To replace plot in his fragmented and logically discontinuous poetic work, he juxtaposed fragments of verse with anecdotes and excerpts from historical documents, rationalizing his poetic long-windedness in this way:

The virtue of strength lies not in the grossness of the fibre, but in the fibre itself. Thus a poem is tough by no quality it borrows from a logical recital of events nor from the event itself, but solely from that attenuated power which draws perhaps many broken things into a dance giving them thus a full being.

The fragmented epic or collage, for Williams, brings about a marriage of heaven and hell, of the epic and the image.

2.

Williams' marriage of image and epic in the fragmented collage of *Paterson* represents a formal discovery that certainly opens up the possibilities of the long poem in our time; and it's a marriage that should be supported and celebrated. In other words, the poetics of the long poem should concern itself less with debating the relative merits of linear and non-linear forms than with discovering the strategies necessary, or useful, in holding a reader's attention over many pages. This certainly seems to have been the primary concern of Michael Ondaatje, Yevgeny Yevtushenko, and Nazim Hikmet, three twentieth-century poets who have dared to go the distance. Ondaatje is on record as disapproving of the distinctions between literary genres and encouraging a more general (and generous) interest in writing as an impulse that may take several directions at once——the poetic, the fictional, and the dramatic. Not surprisingly, his major excursion into the long poem or narrative, *The Collected Works of Billy the Kid*, employs not only a variety of forms of writing, including rhymed verse, anecdotal verse, expository prose, chunks of dialogue, and interviews, but also a narrative, or authorial, stance that is many-sided. It suggests at once, notions of the poet as biographer, collector, recorder and interpreter, and notions of the poet as salvage worker, recovering the legend—i.e., the deeds—of Billy the Kid. The strength of his poem is directly related to his ability to orchestrate all of these elements so that we are interested in story, texture, and meaning.

In his Author's Preface to *Bratsk Station*, Yevtushenko appears slightly apologetic for his long and not-so-easily-defined work:

> Strictly speaking, perhaps, this is not a poem, but simply meditations, joined together by the controversy between two themes: the theme of disbelief in the monologue of the pyramid, and the theme of faith. To some readers the abundance of historical sequences in a poem with such a modern name may seem strange. But at Bratsk, I thought not only of the heroic labours of the builders of the power station but of all the sons and daughters of Russia who have given their lives in the battle for the realization of the highest ideals of humanity ... .

A great deal of weight rests on Yevtushenko's use of the word 'perhaps'; obviously, he considers himself the author of an important poem, however difficult it might be of description or definition. He also knows, from the study of literature of the past, that an aside is by no means always an affront. "It is not by accident," he adds, "that I have made so many historical digressions ... ."

Turkish poet Nazim Hikmet was faced with the same dilemma years earlier, having created a work that breaks all the modernist rules. *Human Landscapes* is a vast, sprawling poem that is part documentary, part biography, part political tract, part stage-play, part dream. In his letters, Hikmet tries to explain his poetic strategies, only to conclude:

Landscapes is not a poetry book. It has elements of poetry and sometimes even technical stuff like rhymes, etc. But it also has elements of prose and drama and even movie scenarios. And what determines the character of the whole, the dominant factor, is not the element of poetry. But it's not any of the others, either. I'm trying to say that I've stopped being a poet; I've become something else.

Hikmet had clearly not stopped being a poet. He had simply assumed the ancient function of poet as historian, moralist, entertainer, prankster, and scribe. He had abandoned the limitations of the lyric tradition, as it had evolved in this century, and staked out claims to territory that had been taken over by other genres. "I'm writing fifty lines a day," he said.

It will be finished in six months and have 10,000 lines ... . I pass my days in uninterrupted work from 8:30 a.m. to midnight, and I am happy. *Landscapes* is proceeding full speed ahead. It's getting longer and longer, but what can I do? Life is so various, people and their lives are so curious, and I am so greedy, so eager to put it all in one book, that I can never call an end to it.

Hikmet's poem grew to 17,000 lines and is one of the great achievements of our time. Perhaps the fact that it was written entirely within the confines of a prison cell has something to do with the force of his rejection of the restrictions of the lyric.

According to Mutlu Konuk, one of Hikmet's editors and translators, the poet's chief concern in his preface to the 1962 Russian translation was quite simple and modest: "I'm curious about just one thing. As you watch these pictures flash past, will you be bored or not." Hikmet's concern about audience response is not surprising, given his sense of having gone on and on, perhaps beyond the bounds of literary propriety. His remarks bring to mind something that Louis Zukovsky said in 1968, while talking about the overall musical structure of the long poem *A*:

I feel that life makes the curve. That's why Williams kept adding to *Paterson*, he found he had more and more to say and that it was all part of the poem. (You know, the poet is insatiable. I could go on talking forever.) Otherwise, you get down to the old argument, there is no such thing as a long poem; there are some good lines and so forth. Maybe, I don't know. A long poem is merely more of a good thing, shall I put it that way? So the nice thing is, for instance, that Pound's *Cantos* are still coming out.

I agree with Zukovsky that the long poem is, at the very least, more of a good thing; that is why I have argued so often for the expansiveness of the narrative tradition and its roots in the epic. There is nothing literary that the long poem should not be able to do; it needn't surrender its powers to the drama or the short story or the novel, just because those forms are currently in favour with the reading public and academia, or because a group of contemporary poets has lost both its powers of narrative and its belief in character and community. And yet, the chorus of dissent to my view remains vigorous. Galway Kinnell has gone on record as saying that "if only a poem could be free of narrative altogether, it would at least open the possibility that some truth could be said directly rather than by parable." Robin Blaser warns against the "grid of meaning" carried in the narrative; Robert Kroetsch, speaking of the "gap between language and narrative," proposes that

> The problem for the writer of the contemporary long poem is to honour our disbelief in belief—that is, to recognize and explore our distrust of system, of grid, of monisms, of cosmologies perhaps, certainly of inherited story—and at the same time write a long work that has some kind of (under erasure) unity";

and Frank Davey, in a similar vein:

> I see narrative as still the central issue of the form. Sequential narrative is an organized system, a language, a structure of signs that speaks of certain assumptions about reality: that it is linear, directed by cause and effect, excluding in its constructions and focuses. In distrust of such assumptions writers have attempted to replace narrative as the long poem's dominant sign.

The degree of epistemological unease (embedded in these references to truth, belief, system, and signs) reminds me of the debates early in the twentieth century about the limitations of the traditional realist-naturalist novel for depicting the great stream of consciousness, the hidden stream of life that surges beneath the thin veneer of manners. What writers such as Conrad, Ford and Virginia Woolf offered as a substitute was but another form of realism, an intensely stylized fiction that brought to the processes of the mind and heart the same attention that novelists had previously brought to action, gesture and speech; in other words, the new doctrine they offered was a kind of psychological realism. As a result, the novelists disrupted sequential narrative, moving back and forth in time; they abandoned the stance of omniscient narration for multiple narrators or a single ironic narrator who might deepen the impact of a story by throwing doubt on its veracity or reliability. The poets I have quoted above seem concerned to fight the same battles over again, as if the war against the strict sequential narrative had not already been fought and won.

While I am sympathetic to those poets who wish to try alternatives to sequential narration, I cannot take seriously their statements that story-telling is somehow aesthetically and morally reprehensible. Robert Kroetsch, who tells and untells great tales in his fiction, tries to limit the poet's function by disallowing the very freedoms he takes in his novels. Perhaps he feels, along with Kinnell, that he is closer to so-called truth when he is writing poetry, though any reader of his wonderful creations will detect a high component of bullshit and playfulness as the poet tries to create, discover and project an image of the 'true' self.

Not long ago, I encountered a statement in a book called *Teaching as a Subversive Activity* which seems to me to illustrate rather nicely the contradiction that is inherent in the present argument against narrative. According to the authors,

One of Marshall McLuhan's insistent themes has been that the electric age has heightened our perceptions of structure by disrupting what he calls the linearity of information flow ... without the distraction of a story line we get a very high involvement in the *forms* of communication, which is another way of saying the processes of learning ... . The focus of intellectual energy becomes the active investigation of structures and relationships, rather than the passive reception of someone else's story.

When I first underlined this comment in my copy of the text, I thought it interesting enough to photocopy for my students in a prose workshop in fiction, to encourage discussion and, perhaps, to get them thinking about alternate structures and about the question of how people read literature. However, I now see the passage in quite a different light.

At first glance, it would seem that the authors offer an attractive argument against the use of narrative in poetry, which is being equated with the use of systems of belief in the classroom. Who could argue against involving readers more vigorously in the medium which, so we are told, is, after all, the real message? Certainly, this version of McLuhan is in cahoots with our postmodern preoccupations with the heightening of structure and the foregrounding of language, especially after decades of criticism in which literature has been milked for its ideas and themes with no apparent awareness that form and content are inextricably allied. The generation raised on *Sesame Street* on television, with its jump-cuts, its discrete fragments, and its zany organizational processes, should have less trouble with Eliot's *Waste Land* fragments, or Prufrockian soliloquies, than might its parents. Six plots running simultaneously in *Hill Street Blues* no longer trouble us; in fact, we regard straightforward narration as rather quaint.

There are a number of misconceptions embedded in these remarks that deserve to be addressed. First, it's not correct to equate story with linearity, since stories may be told in a hundred different ways, including back to front, as Rudy Wiebe does in "Where is the Voice Coming From?" When Conrad, Ford, James and Joyce declared that life, as it is perceived and recalled, does not happen in a straight line, but in bits and pieces most often out of chronological sequence, they did not abandon narrative, but transformed it; so, too, did ancient and medieval poets understand the value of so-called digressions and alienating devices to vary rhythm and increase involvement in the text and its strategies long before Brecht explored these principles in his plays. Poetry will continue to be licensed for subversion, not so much for avoiding systems and structures as for using and altering them; any subversion of word order, any revolt in the halls of grammar, punctuation and diction calls to mind that which is being subverted, challenges our sloppy thinking and feeling, causing us to reassess, readjust and restructure, certainly not to take substance or form for granted.

All poetry, whether narrative, descriptive, lyrical, meditative, documentary or imagistic, is someone's story. The words we use and the feelings that produce them constitute our story and are coloured by what we are and what we know. In the case of very fine poets, though, the story takes on the character and proportions of myth and becomes not just someone else's story, but our own, the story of us all. The entire poem, not just the obviously narrative elements within it, emerges as our story, a metaphorical structure for the world as we see it, from which anyone can deduce how we think the world ought to be. It's foolish to pretend that literature, or education for that matter, could be improved by eliminating story or narrative. Deification of process seems to me doomed to the same hollowness we've witnessed in narrowly thematic approaches to literature or extreme subject-orientation in the classroom.

Fear of narrative seems to be related to our fear of belief. But we need not fear belief, for what is belief but praxis, ideas-in-motion? The poem or work of art is the ultimate symbol of belief-in-motion: it is an act of faith on the part of the creator and that act of faith is relived and repeated each time the work is experienced anew. From the experience of someone's story, whatever the balance of narrative, linguistic and structural elements, comes new knowledge, from which our own story is revised and rewritten. And so it goes. Without this acknowledgement, we are doomed to poverty, in the classroom as well as in poetry. The teacher who is afraid to say "I believe" and the poet who cannot construct an imaginative world which implies "This is how I see our situation at this moment in time," end up transmitting the idea that there is nothing to be known, only points of view or processes to be considered and that knowledge is no more than efficient research and filing. And that, too, constitutes a story, however hollow. How can the teacher or poet, thus reduced, not lose his credibility as a moral force in society and avoid being seen as a mere dabbler in words and ideas? If he or she refuses to make use of story, or narrative, because of its freight of meaning, which is, by definition, tentative, he may be denying himself access to one of poetry's greatest sources of strength, for there is nothing more powerful than metaphor and parable in the literary arsenal. Although I might not take the argument quite so far, I cannot help offering at this point in the discussion Wendell Berry's provocative statement on the subject of narrative in his essay, "The Specialization of Poetry":

But this weakening of narrative in poetry—whether by policy, indifference, or debility—may be one of the keys to what is wrong with us, both as poets and as people. It is indicative of a serious lack of interest, first, in action, and second, in responsible action. Muir said that 'the story, though it is our story, is disappearing from poetry.' Narrative poetry records, contemplates, hands down the actions of the past. Poetry has a responsibility to remember and to preserve and reveal the truth about these actions. But it also has a complementary responsibility that is equally public: to help preserve and to clarify the possibility of responsible action. Ezra Pound, perhaps more than anyone else in our time, insisted on this as the social value of the damned and despised literati. 'When their work goes rotten ... when their very medium, the very essence of their work, the application of word to things goes rotten, i.e. becomes slushy and inexact, or excessive and bloated, the whole machinery of social and of individual thought and order goes to pot.' The word *order* as used here clearly refers to the possibility of responsible action, the possibility of good work.

But our malaise, both in our art and in our lives, is that we have lost sight of the possibility of right or responsible action. Publicly, we have delegated our capacity to act to men who are capable of action only because they cannot think. Privately, as in much of our poetry, we communicate by ironic or cynical allusions to that debased tale of futility, victimization, and defeat, which we seem to have elected to be our story.

Nothing seems to me more counter-productive at this moment in history than to try closing the doors to the past we so desperately need to examine. Let the poets truncate, or disrupt, their narratives, so that they happen in pieces, in reverse, or at random; they may even fragment the narrative or pare it down to the point that what is left seems little more than remnants, not the whole cloth. But let them continue to work with narrative in all its possibilities. As Ezra Pound has advised in *ABC of Reading*,

Narrative sense, narrative power, can survive ANY truncation. If a man have the tale to tell and can keep his mind on that and refuses to worry about his own limitations, the reader will, in the long and short run, find him ... .

E. J. Pratt's truncations of narrative, like those of Hikmet, Ondaatje and Yevtushenko, which include historical digressions. Epic similes or asides, shifts of attention from one character to another, flashbacks, and a host of other less obvious changes of form in terms of diction and music, serve only to deepen the resonance and heighten the impact of the narratives. Like a good playwright or creator of short fictions, Pratt knows intuitively the dramatic value of set-up and pay-off, when to introduce and withhold information, how to create suspense. In the fact of such versatility within the genre, it is surprising to find poets and critics so suspicious of the shape powers of narrative. When Blaser calls narrative "a-historical, a lie," and Kroetsch objects to the "grammar of inherited story" because it is a "mistelling," one is struck by the essential Puritanism of their stance. The hesitation, the fear, and, finally, the impotence of the position is not lost on Kroetsch, whose piece on the long poem is subtitled "foreplay without entrance."

Yeats once described the process by which poems get longer and longer:

A little lyric evokes an emotion, and this emotion gathers others about it and melts into their being in the making of a great epic; and at last, needing an always less delicate body, or symbol, as it grows more powerful, it flows out, with all it has gathered among the blind instincts of daily life, where it moves a power within powers, as one sees ring within ring in the stem of an old tree.

The long poem as a form of branching out, moving out on a limb, and perhaps needing strength of fibre more than fineness or polish. That is how I read poems such as Earle Birney's "November Walk Near False Creek Mouth," Louis Dudek's "Atlantis" and "En Mexico", Stuart

McKinnon's "The Intervals," Don McKay's "Long Sault," Daphne Marlatt's "Steveston", Robert Kroetsch's "Seed Catalogue," and "Stone Hammer Poem," Frank Davey's "King of Swords", Henry Beissel's "Season of Blood" and George Bowering's "Kerrisdale Elegies"—all growing out of that single emotion and building thereon, following the tradition of meditations on history and place that includes "The Deserted Village," "Tintern Abbey," and "The Height of Land." The object of attention may be a moment in the poet's personal or collective history, but it might also be a fragment of biography: Phyllis Webb's sequence of poems on the stripped psyche, Dorothy Livesay's documentary on the evacuation of the Japanese-Canadians, and D.G. Jones's touching sequence on the love-affair of Archibald Lampman and Kate. Anything will do that stimulates the ear and eye and imagination to create. As. W. C. Williams said in another context: "Local colour is not, as the parodists, the localists, believe an object of art. It is merely a variant serving to locate the acme point of white penetration." Narrative or autobiography are also variants that help the poet find his or her true focus.

Kroetsch and Pratt are not so far apart, after all. They both recognize that the long poem, to hold our attention, must employ every trick in the book and invent some new ones. "Seed Catalogue" and "Towards the Last Spike" both aim to educate and entertain, both insist on moving beyond the particulars of story, biography or history that gave them rise towards generalizations about society, nation and, ultimately, about art and language as well. Milton Wilson's remarks about Pratt's narrative apply equally well to the long poems of Kroetsch or, for that matter, to Ondaatje's *The Collected Works of Billy the*

Kid; such poets write "narratives no doubt, but discontinuous narratives which are always turning, on the one side, into documents, letters, and jokes and on the other, into pure lyrics."

The task of criticism will be to bring as much attention to bear on the long poem in all its manifestations as has been showered on the lyric and on the novel. My own experience of writing and studying the long poem suggests that pacing and duration are key concerns, knowing when to change gears and how fast to go. *War & Other Measures*, which is ostensibly a fictionalization of the life and death of Paul Joseph Chartier, the so-called mad bomber of the House of Commons, is, in fact, a cultural manifesto which departs from the truth of fact in terms of Chartier's life in order to arrive at the psychological truth of his final gesture as a Canadian martyr/fool. The only way I could handle this material was to create a diary, or journal, of what might be called approximate sonnets, from five to twenty-five lines, with varying degrees of compression and closure, courting but never fully embracing the prosaic. Frye has mentioned a facet of the long poem or narrative that also deserves attention in this context: "We tend to form our canons of criticism on carefully polished poetry, but such standards do not always apply to the narrative, for the test of a great narrative is its ability to give the flat prose statement a poetic value." I don't know exactly what Frye meant here, but I do know that my own work, by shattering the narrative into discrete fragments, or remnants, each of which ought to have the coherence and impact of a photograph, a stopped-frame in a movie, or a chapter in a novel, the most straightforward statement can be made to resonate with meaning far beyond expectations.

There's much to be learned about the long poem, and too much that needs to be written that requires this larger canvas, for us to waste any more time talking nonsense about the impossibility and unsuitability of narrative. What Frye had to say about Canadian narratives should be applied to the long poem generally: "... there are many failures and many errors of taste and stretches of bad writing, but to anyone who cares about poetry there may be something more interesting in the failure than in a less ambitious success."

Sources:

Yevgeny Yevtushenko, *Bratsk Station and Other New Poems*; Nazim Hikmet, *Human Landscapes*; Louis Zukovsky, quoted in *Contemporary Literature*; Wendell Berry, in Reginald Gibbons (ed.), *The Poet's Work*; Robin Blaser in Michael Ondaatje (ed.) *The Long Poem Anthology*; Robert Kroetsch, *The Lovely Treachery of Words*; Neil Postman and Charles Weingartner, *Teaching as A Subversive Activity*; Ezra Pound, *ABC of Reading*; W.B. Yeats, "The Symbolism of Poetry" in *Collected Essays of W. B. Yeats*; Northrop Frye, *The Bush Garden*.

4: Catching Dogs: Ondaatje's *Tin Roof*

Discussion of the Canadian long poem, some of which took place at the "The Coast Is Only A Line" conference at Simon Fraser University and "The Long-Liners" conference at York University, has focussed, according to Eli Mandel, primarily on two issues, genre and structure. "Genre," he says, provides

> ...a metaphysics of beginnings. It sustains the long poem in the form of the epic, those encyclopaedic narratives at the fountainhead of western culture. As a narrative poem of heroic action, the epic was intended to encompass, to give shape and purpose to all learning, striving to become the definitive poem of its age. When the containing form collapsed, shortly after but not because of Milton, it broke into its two component parts, narrative and encyclopaedic poem, the long poem. The history of the long poem is largely the history of its search for a structural principle to replace the heroic narrative of choice and action.

While I don't agree with Mandel's division of the field into narrative and encyclopaedic poem, I think he is more or less correct about the flight from one kind of narrative and the search for alternative structures. *Narrative*, of course, is a problematical term. If you look at the etymology of the term *narrative* in the *O.E.D.*, you will find that the word was often used as a pejorative to mean verbosity, chattiness, the condition we might now refer to as motor-mouth, and it was ungenerously associated with female talkers. Fortunately, narrative has come into its own as a much broader, more flexible and inclusive term, referring less to causally-linked events in a text than to the obvious or submerged stories and value-systems embedded in most verbal structures.

Michael Ondaatje has been a pioneer of the long poem in Canada, beginning with two traditional short narratives, "Elizabeth" and "Peter," and quickly moving out into uncharted terrain with two book-length long poems, *The Man With Seven Toes* and *The Collected Works of Billy the Kid*, and, more recently, *Tin Roof*. He is also the editor of the first edition of *The Long Poem Anthology*, published by Coach House Press. Although *Billy the Kid* is a touchstone for those who wish to know what can be achieved in the long poem, Ondaatje, like another of his contemporaries, Robert Kroetsch, has managed to nurse a crisis of confidence in the efficacy of poetry as a vehicle for sustained narration, while at the same time launching himself on a successful career as a writer of prose fiction. The resulting double standard, which permits narrative in fiction but not in poetry, has, at worst, delayed a full critical appreciation of the Canadian long poem in all its manifestations; at best, it has driven poets to considerable lengths in search of structural alternatives to narrative, or story. While pursuing his overt story-telling impulses under the banner of prose fiction, Ondaatje's search for alternative structural principles in poetry has taken him, in his long poem *Tin Roof*, back to the ode, particularly the romantic ode, and to such extended meditative poems of the Nineteenth Century as "The Prelude" and "Dover Beach."

In terms of a metaphysics of origins, *Tin Roof* can be usefully traced back to the romantic odes, those wonderful testaments to survival that begin with Wordsworth's "Dejection: An Ode" (1802), "Tintern Abbey," and "Ode: Intimations of Immortality" (1802-4), Shelley's "Ode to the West Wind", and Keats's "Ode On A Grecian Urn." The classical Pindaric ode is a hymn in praise of, often exalted and intense, celebrating victories and special occasions and using whatever seems appropriate from the roster of divine myths; the Horatian ode, as described in the *Princeton Encyclopedia of Poetry & Poetics*, tends to be "personal rather than public, general rather than occasional, tranquil rather than intense, contemplative rather than brilliant, and intended for the reader in his library rather than for the spectator in the theatre." The romantic ode, a significant variation on the theme, marries this hymn of praise to a narrative of personal recovery, the sad, beleaguered, creatively-blocked, and perhaps suicidal poet relates how he has been transformed by an encounter with a strikingly unusual place in nature, a thing of beauty, a woman, or some other natural or man-made phenomenon. In Canada, the romantic ode, which I call the manic-depressive ode, has had an interesting history, being employed by such diverse talents as D. C. Scott in "A Height of Land" and Earle Birney, most notably in "Cartagena de Indias" and "A Walk in Kyoto." In the latter, Birney recalls being an uncomprehending, awkward, and over-sized Gulliver in Japan's discreet, highly refined society, but suddenly glimpsing a possible window of integration through witnessing and sharing the maid's delight in the flight of a carp-shaped kite, a symbol of the transcendental power of the imagination. In "Cartagena," he is a well-heeled gringo, feeling displaced, guilty, and uninspired on the poverty-ridden streets of South America, but whose spirits are miraculously resurrected by the discovery of a statue to the shoes of Colombian poet Luis Lopez:

> I love the whole starved cheating
> poetry reading lot of you most of all
> for throwing me the shoes of deadman Luis

to walk me back into your brotherhood.

Of course, the dice are always loaded in such post-facto accounts, which have a way of shifting from confessions to manifestos, and "Cartagena" is no exception, since Birney manages to get in a few digs about how, poverty or not, poets are better-loved in Colombia than in Vancouver, where, he says, I "am seldom read by my countrymen."

Tin Roof, a fascinating variation on the romantic ode, is a long poem in sixteen parts, which begins with a faint fragment from the narrative of self that includes an admission of being too busy, no longer knowing what to say, and possibly suicidal:

> You stand still for three days
> for a piece of wisdom
> and everything falls to the right place
>
> or wrong place
>
> > > You speak
> > don't know whether
> seraph or bitch
> flutters at your heart
>
> and look through windows
> for cue cards
> blazing in the sky.
> > > The solution.
> > This last year I was sure
> > I was going to die.

It's a tantalizing fragment, for its Wordsworthian notion of the world being too much with us, and its, for Ondaatje, uncharacteristically confessional note, but also for the theatrically self-aware image of cue cards and the pun implied by his usage of the word *place*: things don't fall *into* place, which would be the conventional usage, but fall *to a place*, which we learn, right off, contains a window.

Tin Roof will obviously not be simply a hymn in praise of physical landscape or place, as the second section makes immediately clear, directing our attentions to "the geography of this room" which the poet has presumably memorized. The place is a small cabin made of glass and wood—"tin bucket on the Pacific rim"—which contains a table he can find in the dark to write on and is situated in a place of warm rains. Since geckoes climb the glass to peer into the room and a "tirade" of waves pound volcanic rock nearby, we assume a location more like Hawaii than Vancouver Island.

The theatrical image of looking for cue cards "blazing in the sky", which appears in section one and, along with the mention of "whisperings," serves as a playful nod to the epic tradition of invoking the muse, is recalled in section two, where ocean and land are set up as antagonists in a drama that leaves the waves, like their observer, "falling to pieces." In section three, these same waves are up to their tricks again leaping at the cliff, but this time perceived less as an attack than as part of a natural rhythm of advance and retreat that the speaker identifies with, the "unknown magic" he throws himself into and which, with a nod to Wallace Stevens and his guitar, is significantly and humorously called "the blue heart", both the site of his psychic drowning and his still-to-come imaginative recovery.

While various narrative threads—place, the self, and writing—have been introduced, section three announces a fourth thread, the erotic: the image of the speaker rising from his "peninsula of sheets" on the bed and wandering in a loose green kimono to the window where he can look past the persistent and by now familiar gecko and the appropriately named deadfall at the sea, and recall in a parenthetical aside either his own or someone else's barroom observation:

> (How to drive
> the Hana Road, he said—
> one hand on the beer
> one hand on your thigh
> and one eye for the road)

The erotic component will come as no surprise to readers of Ondaatje's work, who will recall moments of extraordinary sensuality, from the bones Billy the Kid sees moving in the wrist of a friend's wife to the exotic couplings of the English patient with his colleague's wife.

Tin Roof is as much a hymn to the erotic as it is to the sea, to solitude, and to the healing powers of poetry. While the poet continues to detail the particulars of place, adding a fridge of beer and mangoes, bamboo, tin roof, "a wind run radio", ceramic chimes, orange flowers with a drunken demeanour, and banana trees, he gradually introduces the presence of woman, the erotic *other*, first by her absence, then by an amazingly particular heightening of sensory detail, which includes the gecko whose "tiny leather toes / hug the glass" and waves that "touch" the volcano, until, in the ninth section, he gives in to direct recall:

> There was the woman
> who clutched my hair
> like a shaken child.

In a passage that remarkably blends sea and communication in the image of "a lost wave length"—and suggests volumes by way of indirection— woman, sea, wind, pebble, and death itself are fused, so that the speaker, who has found himself transparent and disintegrating, "joyous and breaking down", is able to immerse himself in the memory of erotic experience, both personal and cinematic:

> Remember
> those women in movies
> who wept into the hair
> of their dead men?

Here, and in the tenth section, physical place gives way entirely to Eros, love's body, which includes a memory of the beloved bracing her feet on the ceiling during sex, with "the sea in her eye", and a delightfully humorous domestic moment of mapping the body:

> Good
> morning to your body
> hello nipple
> and appendix scar like a letter
> of too much passion
> from a mad Mexican doctor
>
> All this noise at your neck!
>
> heart clapping

It's difficult here, and elsewhere in the poem, to know precisely who is being referred to. The speaker has previously referred to himself as *I, you*, and *he*; here he begins with *I*, refers to *her*, then, after a cleverly placed distraction on truffles, culinary art, and a text called *Physiologie du Gout* (which I first mistakenly read as gout rather than the French word for taste), he shifts to a second-person address, which could refer to himself or to the beloved, since both will have been restored by the encounter, but which turns out to refer to the beloved, now even further merged with the sea by virtue of "this earring / which / has flipped over / and falls / into the pool of your ear." There's a great deal of compression at work here. Above the lovers are blazing sky, wind, tin roof, and bamboo, an instrument used not only for construction, but also for torture and war; below them, potential destruction, from rocks and the ever-present volcano. The erotic, like the sea, protects the lovers from loneliness and from "the burning red river" of lava that runs under earth and sea.

I don't have the space here to trace the development of all the narrative threads in *Tin Roof*, but I want to suggest how carefully and deliberately the poem has been constructed. I'm reminded by Ondaatje's erotic imagery of both the traditional ode's link with athletic victories and Dionysiac theatre and of Peter Brooks' attempts to define a sexual dynamic at work in all narrative. In *Reading for the Plot: Design and Intention in Narrative*, he defines plot as

the organizing line and intention of narrative, thus perhaps best conceived as an activity, a structuring operation elicited in the reader trying to make sense of those meanings that develop only through textual and temporal succession.

"Narratives," he insists, "both tell of desire ... and arouse and make use of desire as dynamic of signification." He also speaks of the need to tell as

a primary human drive that seeks to seduce and to subjugate the listener, to implicate him in the thrust of a drive that can never quite speak its name—never can quite come to the point—but that insists on speaking over and over again its movement toward that name.

Certainly, there is more than enough evidence in *Tin Roof* to suggest that Ondaatje is a master of narrative arousal.

With the healing effects of erotic love permeating the text, inspiration begins to return to the poet. References to death recede into the background to be replaced by verbal playfulness; the tight-lipped imagism gives way to a philosophizing attitude; and an encyclopaedic range of reference invades the poem, to include mapping, bathyspheres, cameo appearances by Bogart, Burt Lancaster, and even John Berryman, with the bite of his suicide—"doing the Berryman walk"— transformed into a metaphor for geological exploration. What comes to dominate the poem at the end, however, is not an evocation of place or erotic love, but a tribute to the genius—I suppose one might say, here, *genus*, since it is located so specifically in one species—of the poet Rainer Maria Rilke.

For anyone unfamiliar with the poem, this shift may come as a surprise, since I have so far deliberately avoided any mention of Rilke. Ondaatje employs a similar strategy, of course, except for little signals along the way, such as the reference to *seraphs* in section one and the bird sounds represented as *duino,* in section nine. Once the secret is out of the bag, however, students of Rilke will have a hay-day with the poem, since mood, cliffside location, references to love and sex and cooking and circus acrobats and the idea that "every place has its own wisdom" all speak of Rilke and *Duino Elegies*. Not surprisingly, given the model I have suggested of the contemporary romantic ode—and, of course, the traditional elegy, which this can be seen as a variation on (the near-death of the poet himself replacing the death of another as subject), *Tin Roof* becomes a hymn in praise of creativity in general, poetry in particular. The poet becomes loquacious, even effusive, like someone loosened up by friends, goodwill, and a few drinks at a party; he dreams up a poetic explanation for the sea-bottom and the strange formations of the earth he has found himself camped on; he becomes determined to be happy *and* to write, a proposition that he had initially seen as an either/or. And, of course, he introduces his own version of the Rilkean angels, dead creatures (poets, lovers, animals, movie stars) aspiring to influence and guide us and, perhaps, alter the face of the land.

 Tin Roof is a playful, if deadly serious, long poem. For those who know the poet, it is an invitation to reconstruct a stretch of that unofficial biography we call the narrative of self. For those who know how Ondaatje loves to play with shapes and allusions, there is the obvious game of literary reference—guess who I'm writing from and about?—comically admitted in the parenthetical aside in section thirteen:

> (Listen, solitude, X wrote,
> is not an absolute,
> it is just a resting place)

In the interests of arousal and delay, Ondaatje refuses to name either the loved one or his literary influence at the outset, but when he does name the latter we are forced to smile at the lengths he has gone both to seed the text with clues and to veil the reference, to the point of furnishing the cabin with a fridge to put Rainier beer into, which he can later recall when he apologizes to Rilke for taking his name slumming among the detritus of quotidian reality.

The sixteenth and final section of the poem is a poignant and instructive site of identification between the speaker and Rilke, where all the elements of the poem come together—place, writing, Eros, and the self, not to forget busyness, bamboo, wisdom, maps, private angels, drowning, and dogs. What Ondaatje work would be complete without dogs? He begins by wondering if the seraph whispering in his ear might, instead, be a bitch. He quotes Rilke's line: "I howl at the moon / with all my heart / and put the blame / on the dogs." And, lest he has given insufficient space to these creatures, he even introduces a perhaps out-of-context dogwood flower, which is said to resemble a woman's sex. Other literary ancestors and familiars are there, too. There is an only slightly veiled allusion to Eliot's Prufrock in the green hair of the waves being combed; a possible drunken allusion to Baudelaire; and an unmistakable Conradian allusion about letting yourself drown in that notorious destructive element, the sea. The whole conclusion is so cleverly and artfully orchestrated that it enables the poem to end on, and fully support, four abstractions, surely a risk even the most gifted of poets would be reluctant to take. Thus woman, writing, and self come together, along with idea of poem as map, circus, and password, in a final apotheosis:

> As at midnight we remember the colour
> of the dogwood flower growing
> like a woman's sex outside the window.
> I wanted poetry to be walnuts
> in their green cases
> but now it is the sea
> and we let it drown us,
> and we fly to it released

> by giant catapults
> of pain loneliness deceit and vanity

As does the conclusion of the romantic ode, *Tin Roof* celebrates the recovery of creative powers. The writerly references that abound in this long poem are worth another word in closing, as they provide a clue both to Ondaatje's attraction to Rilke and his developing poetic strategies. The aesthetic of this poem moves between silence and eloquence. The poet announces early that, although he does not know what to say, he prefers the quietude of the bamboo hut, where there is "not a word", only the sound of water dripping from a bamboo pipe, and the birds "who / tchick tchick tchick / my sudden movement / who say nothing else." He proposes to "avoid a story" in favour of those numerous details and narrative remnants he provides. Against the "slack-key" music on the radio, he places the "words and music entangled in pebble / ocean static." Like Rilke and, I presume, most postmodern poets who are at war with eloquence, he insists:

> I want the passion
> which puts your feet on the ceiling
> this fist
> to smash forward
>
> take this silk
>   somehow *Ah*
> out of the rooms of poetry

This is a reassertion of Robert Herrick's dictum that a poet should aim for "a sweet disorder in the dress", an image that appears more explicitly in *The English Patient*.

In his introduction to the first edition of *The Long Poem Anthology*, Ondaatje stresses the elements of process and discovery that he admires in the writing of the contemporary long poem:

The poets do not fully know what they are trying to hold until they near the end of this poem, and this uncertainty, this lack of professional intent, is what allows them to go deep. The poems have more to do with open fields and quiet rooms than public stages ... These poets listen to everything. Kroetsch hangs around bars picking up stories like Polonius behind the curtain, others recall childhood language, or hold onto dreams after they have awakened, or speak the unsaid politics of the day. They tempt quiet things out of the corner. 'It is not easy to catch dogs when it is your business to catch dogs,' said Steinbeck.

It's intriguing and, I think, instructive to see how close this statement is in phrasing and sentiment to the lines quoted earlier on the Horatian ode from the *Princeton Encylopedia of Poetry & Poetics*: "... intended for the reader in his library rather than for the spectator in the theatre." While he may resist conventional forms, may prefer to begin without knowing where the poem will take him, and may struggle to avoid story, Ondaatje's *Tin Roof* certainly defies the word "unprofessional", which he applies to his favourite long poems. Although he courts the anecdotal, the discursive, the colloquial, the seemingly extraneous, even the banal, the narrative threads of *Tin Roof*, which I have only touched upon here, are subtly and intricately woven. The poem, partaking of the openness and malleability of the romantic ode, is fascinating for the way in which it walks a tightrope between the private and the public, moving from personal, parochial detail to a high romantic, one might even say theatrical, pitch, juggling children, gymnastic lovers, geckoes, beer cans, and dogs. The strategy, which involves rewriting while deconstructing the conventional ode, is not entirely new— in fact, it was anticipated by Wordsworth in "Tintern Abbey," which, as Antony Easthope says, "gives the effect of the presence of the speaker by denying its presence as a poem"—but Ondaatje's results are thoroughly contemporary and engaging.

In *Tin Roof*, many ideas and quiet things are tempted, like geckoes, out of the corner, including what some readers might call the fetishization of women, where the male poetic mentor is named but the human beloved is not. However, lest I transgress too far from the spirit of *Tin Roof*, I will end with that famous quotation from Rilke which appears under the mast-head of *Brick*, the magazine Ondaatje edits with his companion Linda Spalding: "Works of art are of an infinite loneliness and with nothing to be so little appreciated as with criticism. Only love can grasp and hold and fairly judge them."

Sources:
Open Letter: Long-Liners Conference Issue, Sixth Series, Nos. 2-3, Summer-Fall 1985; Alex Preminger (ed.), *The New Princeton Encyclopedia of Poetry and Poetics*; note on Earle Birney in *15 Canadian Poets*; Peter Brooks, *Reading for the Plot*; Ondaatje, *The Long Poem Anthology*; Anthony Easthope, *Poetry As Discourse*.

5: The Machinery of Desire: Sharon Thesen's *Confabulations*

In *Reading for the Plot: Design and Intention in Narrative* (1984), Peter Brooks speaks of the "narrative motor" that drives a text, the fundamental dynamic that stimulates our desire to continue towards recognition and ending. "We can, then, conceive of plot as a form of desire that carries us forward, onward, through the text", he says.

Narratives both tell of desire—typically present some story of desire—and arouse and make use of desire as dynamic of signification. Desire is in this view like Freud's notion of Eros, a force including sexual desire but larger and more polymorphous, which (he writes in *Beyond the Pleasure Principle*) seeks 'to combine organic substances into ever greater unities'.

I'm interested here in the design of Sharon Thesen's long poem *Confabulations* (1984), which explores some of the mysteries surrounding the death of Malcolm Lowry. While it may seem odd to cite a book about the function of plot in the novel, you can see immediately from Brooks' statement how the concept of desire might apply to long poems and poetic narratives, which depend not only on connective tissue (which you need to hold the pieces together), but also on a driving force, whatever serves to maintain momentum, keep us engaged and reading.

I'd like to show how Sharon Thesen in *Confabulations* employs a kind of narrative shorthand, seeding the text with elements of story, with the ghost of a plot (or plots). In the case of many postmodern texts the story component usually involves ostensible 'information' about the author and the process of composition. This is only marginally the case in *Confabulations*, where the material that fuels the narrative motor is drawn mainly from the two fictional works, *Under the Volcano* and *Hear Us O Lord from Heaven Thy Dwelling Place*, and two non-fiction sources, *The Selected Letters of Malcolm Lowry*, edited by Harvey Breit and Margerie Bonner Lowry, and Douglas Day's biography, *Malcolm Lowry*.

By giving us a short prefatory biographical sketch of Lowry's death in Ripe, East Sussex on June 27, 1957, Thesen is able to suggest immediately that this is not a conventional "life" she is writing. In fact, the two small indicators that are intended as clues in the mystery to be unravelled are the possibility of a suicide, by an overdose of alcohol and drugs, and the doctor's diagnosis of "death by misadventure", a phrase which Lowry would have enjoyed. The medical diagnosis, of course, is rendered less than convincing by the accompanying statement that Lowry was "buried just at the edge of consecrated ground in the churchyard".

Having established that she will address this ambiguity, Thesen then offers the reader two epigraphs, including one from Lowry which begins with the straightforward observation, "I still believe that bad French wine was my nemesis", which might be taken literally, but which proceeds with an ironic comment that eliminates any potential for seriousness: "I began to improve slightly when I took to rum and gave up taking vitamins." Lowry acknowledges his own alcoholism, but dismisses its importance. The second epigraph, from Gaston Bachelard's *The Psychoanalysis of Fire*, is more ambiguous in intent.

When the fire devours itself, when the power turns against itself, it seems as if the whole being is made complete at the instant of its final ruin and the intensity of the destruction is the supreme proof, the clearest proof, of its existence.

Fire and alcohol will prove to be dominant images in the poems to follow. Lowry's shack will be consumed by fire; he will have nightmares and hallucinations of hellfire. And the reader will carry, consciously or not, the suggestion created by the use of Bachelard's quotation, that there is a deeper burn at work here for which alcohol is a mere symptom, a burn which positively seeks its own annihilation. Before we have even entered the poem per se, Thesen has created in us a desire to know what killed Lowry and she has suggested that Psychoanalysis might be the most fruitful direction to take. To make sure we haven't missed the point, she next includes Lowry's self-styled epitaph, which appears in his *Selected Poems*:

> Malcolm Lowry
> Late of the Bowery
> His prose was flowery
> And often glowery
> He lived, nightly, and drank, daily,
> And died playing the ukelele.

The lightness of this piece, which ends with the positive image of a writer dying while making music, however silly, should not blind us to the underlying pathos it contains regarding Lowry's self-doubts about his down-and-out life and, more important, about the value of his writing.

Perhaps the most telling image in this playful epitaph is that of Lowry the insomniac, who stays up all night and conducts his life in the dark. *Confabulations* is seeded with frequent references to darkness, building up a picture of someone inordinately attracted to night, madness, and death: we encounter in the poem the "dead / of night", "the dark symbolic horse", the "day of the Dead", the recurring phrase "Where I am it is dark", and the devastating final section with its image of Lowry "sucking mother night". I use the phrase "telling image" deliberately, since this is Thesen's means of providing remnants of narrative, plot, shards of a life that draw us on and keep us engaged as readers trying to piece together the puzzle.

The actual poem begins on an urgent note, a note of alcoholic anxiety, focussing on the internal life, the "silent movie" with its broken "flapping celluloid", the "mind's guts churning / sweating nervous erratic / guilt". We don't know where the guilt comes from, it can't (or won't) be identified, but somehow it leaves Lowry's mind invaded by the outside world, a "fast dissolve / a light snow falling in the room." The uncertain boundaries between self and other, between the receiver-self who suffers and a world that keeps sending its array of sometimes overwhelming messages, will prove central to the poem, resulting in a final loss of identity. Once again, the elements prove central:

> A lot of rain falling
> & wasted days
> but a few gins
> & and I can still get off
> a decent letter.
> My personality comes & goes
> like the mailman, however
> & I can honestly admit
> (at my age, how embarrassing)
> that I have no idea
> who I am. Was always
> good at sea, though.
> Without a storm

I'm useless.

This recalls, of course, the sonnet "Joseph Conrad", where Lowry compares the poet's or fiction writer's struggle with chaos to the sailor's efforts to ride out a storm at sea. Here are the seven final lines:

> What derricks of the soul plunge in his room.
> Yet some mariner's ferment in his blood
> —Though truant heart will hear the iron travail
> And song of ships that ride their easting down—
> Sustains him to subdue or be subdued.
> In sleep all night he grapples with a sail!
> But words beyond the life of ships dream on.

Earlier, we have learned that Lowry feels too much, that his heart lies open, not to *receive* surgery, but to function as a surgical instrument, presumably for us, his readers. At the end, though, all boundaries collapse. The self shifts sideways, like the earlier drunk who kept staggering to the left; the mind explodes; the world, not just alcohol and drugs, is there (or not there) for oral gratification; the elements invade Lowry, so that "earth & stars, fire & sea" are once again inside the writer.

Lowry, as we gather bit by bit, is torn by various conflicts: Lowry the polluted drunk with his "bones poisoned", yet still concerned about rectitude and appearing casual as he makes an unsteady beeline for the hidden bottle, too far gone to stop, but not drunk enough to ignore the possibility that the friend watching him might be experiencing disgust; Lowry the self-destructive romantic, whose spiritual impulses are drowned by alcoholic spirits, which bind and sunder, aid and abet love, are a shortcut to paradise or hell, and cause him to abase himself, to pray and make deals with the saints.

Obviously, Lowry's sexuality troubles him. He feels himself "an amorous snake / in the amorous grass"; pages later, he feels the hellfire at his heels, "panting & fanged" like the serpent, desire.

In section nine, the poem shifts into an analytic mode. Lowry descends into the rag and bone shop, from which position he blames his mother, his nanny, his infamous trip as a child to the Syphilis Museum, and his time in Bellevue Psychiatric Hospital. This descent produces a temporary "boozeless" resurrection. Instead of sitting on the beach, closed tight as a clam, he sees the world, which is now his "oyster", clearly; he can write to publishers, address Margerie with affection, and notice the new curtains she has made, which are not to be confused with the final curtains of the dying butterfly caught in the cat's jaws in section seven. This is a short-lived resurrection, to be sure, followed by a visit to the bootlegger and an ignominious collapse into earth and blackness.

The 'writing body", which we have seen as both "instrument" and "transmitter", begins to break down. The ferris wheel doubling as the wheel of fortune, which dominated *Under the Volcano*, makes its appearance here on the cover and in the text of *Confabulations*, appropriately at 'midway', rotating backwards and carrying a vomiting Lowry. This prefigures another dark night of the soul, bringing on the paranoia of life in Mexico, police, vultures, the death of Marquez, chair rungs visible through the white cotton shirt "like bones", and a lost passport. From here the apocalypse is not far off, with images of a "one-legged rooster / & a sleeping dog" (which the writer obviously can't let lie, at least in one sense of the word), and with Spanish words (the last of which is "thief") intruding and drowning out English. The poem shifts into high-gear as Lowry approaches a state of complete mental collapse, referring literally to jazz and assuming a jazzy improvisational mode, so that the reader can no longer distinguish between the figure of the Consul in *Under the Volcano* and Lowry the man, who dreams of being eaten by women and finds "the whole grief of the world / strangling my words".

The demise of Lowry the writer precipitates the demise of Lowry the man. His rapid unravelling includes mention of his love-hate for Margerie, talk of a lobotomy, memories of a horrendous experiment at his expense in Bellevue, Margerie's half-mad cosmic laughter on the way home from Gabriola Island, and their precipitous departure for England, where Malcolm appears to be rotting away in a village that is called Ripe, where he drinks at a pub called The Lamb and appears himself a lamb for the sacrifice, where he is physically at peace but admits that something has definitely killed the storm in him that he finds so necessary for his writing. Caught in the web of his own fears and nightmares, he recalls the remark made by the assassin of Marquez: "you no wrider / you an espider." Embedded in this whimsical mis-pronunciation are writer/rider and spi/spider parallels. Lowry and his poetic biographer riding the whirlwind and spinning webs of dream.

Thesen has created in *Confabulations* a rich and complex linguistic structure, where signifiers are often subversively coded to do double duty, where narrative and semantic events function referentially but also contain hints, clues, and inconsistencies that render definitive interpretation impossible. In the final section, for example, Thesen's syntactical strategy makes it impossible to know for sure whether the word "sucking" is being used as verb or adjective, whether an orally-deprived Lowry, in dying, is "sucking mother night" or if mother night, which shatters, claims, and detonates, is sucking him, like some sort of cosmic vacuum-cleaner, into its black hole. It's a world Lowry would recognize, abounding with "Correspondences / too creepy to ignore."

Although the word "confabulations" is defined in the *O.E.D.* as ordinary, colloquial talk, the poem and its subject matter are anything but ordinary. In using this word for her title, Thesen is obviously tickling the ribs of critics who now use the word *fabulation* to refer to fiction. Her fragmented, non-linear poem is itself a fable, a "sideways conspiracy" that keeps us guessing; and, while declaring "all things for the mouth / shattered", she renders Lowry's tempestuous life and grotesque dying eloquent, letting out of the bottle of her poetic biography an appropriately playful and elusive genie.

While *Confabulations* does not have plot in the conventional sense, it is carefully plotted, using a structure not unlike that of *Under the Volcano,* in which a death is announced and we proceed meticulously backwards to discover how and why it came to pass. In only twenty-seven brief fragments, Thesen is able to evoke the troubled genius of Lowry, deftly sketch a life, echo the major concerns of his writing, and play her own ukulele rendition of Lowry's brilliant wit and doomed trajectory.

Who is surprised to discover, at the end of *Confabulations,* that the bird which, like a sailor, pipes-in the morning after Lowry's death, is no ordinary songster, but a mockingbird?

Sources:

Sharon Thesen, *Confabulations*; Peter Brooks, *Reading for the Plot*; Gaston Bachelard, *The Psychoanalysis of Fire*; Malcolm Lowry, *Under the Volcano*.

6: Bridging the Narrows: *Falsework*

A faint whiff of diesel permeated the space as members of the audience began to trickle in to the Ocean Cement machine-shop on Granville Island. A dripping sign outside the building announced the production of *Falsework* sponsored by the 2007 Vancouver International Writers Festival. Dave Beatty, head of Ironworkers Local 97, had arrived early and was at the door, a self-appointed welcoming committee. Theatre was not Dave's cup of tea, but he loved the publicity angle and had purchased a block of twenty-five tickets for members and staff. The space was odd but congenial, with none of the usual pretence of a commercial theatre with its lobby-full of wine-sipping patrons; instead, it might have been mistaken for a clandestine meeting of the Wobblies. Oil drums cast shadows against the wall to the right of the raised stage area, simulating an industrial cliff-face. Downstage left several girlie calendars were mounted between huge wrenches and various tools of the heavy-duty mechanic's trade. Although the grease pit and under-body work area would have been ideal for exits, entrances and miraculous disappearances in a full-scale production, safety considerations plus the modest ambitions of a dramatic reading had prompted the company to cover the trench with 4x8 sheets of one-inch plywood, thereby increasing the seating area.

As the audience settled into their chairs, director Martin Kinch whispered a few words of encouragement to the actors from Playwrights Theatre Centre who had spent the better part of two weeks rehearsing *Falsework*, struggling to produce something that resembled a play from a bevy of discontinuous poetic monologues. This required each of the three men and one woman to take on and animate at least half a dozen different voices. I had sat through the painful surgical procedures stoically, amazed as usual at the difference between their talents and my own and wishing I'd had this experience *before* publishing the book. The actors, mounted on four stools, were studying personally annotated versions of the text and trying to ignore the hubbub of voices, the shedding of rain-clothes and the shuffling of chairs on the cement floor of the machine-shop. As the lights were extinguished, a huge image of the Second Narrows Bridge under construction was projected on the wall behind the actors. The bridge rampant and indestructible.

On June 17, 1958, this same bridge collapsed during construction, taking the lives of eighteen workers and, later, a diver. At the time, I was working on the waterfront at BC Sugar Refinery loading boxcars with 100-pound sacks of white sugar, so the news did not take long to reach me.

> . . . God, it was blue, the sky
>
> a currency even the poor could bank
> on. We'd ordered our usual, eggs
> over-easy, with an extra side of toast,
> when the first of five ambulances
>
> shrieked past. It was difficult to imagine
> disaster on such a day, the birds
> singing hallelujah on the wires, clouds
> on strike, growing things amazed
>
> by their own virtuosity, operatic,
> playing the clown. The radio, having
> kept its counsel, suddenly belted out
> the news, interrupting a ballad

by Crosby, something about dreams
dancing. We piled into the street
and moved en masse to the waterfront,
holding our breath, daring our eyes.

I learned later that my father, a former navy diver, had been called out to search for bodies in the wreckage. For decades, I carried the image of him dangling from an umbilical cord of oxygen in that cauldron of swirling water and twisted metal. I recall the shock and disbelief I felt as I ran towards the pier at Buckerfield's Seeds to see for myself the collapsed bridge. The huge girders that moments before had pushed out boldly across Burrard Inlet were now mangled and sloped down into the water. A flotilla of small boats was converging on the spot to pick up bodies and survivors. There was nothing I could do, so I returned to my job and the mountain of sugar sacks at the refinery. The bridge disaster did not stop me in my tracks, but it gave me pause when thinking about the future and about the reliability of those who were shaping that future, building the infrastructures that would carry me into decades ahead. I would never again look at a new building, a bridge or an overpass under construction without that almost imperceptible catch in the breathing that playwrights identify in their scripts as "a beat." Enough of those beats can produce a very cautious, even frightened, person.

* * *

History is long, but the trajectory of a bridge collapse is short, a few seconds and a couple of hundred feet. Its effects, however, embrace a *life-span*. The Second Narrows bridge disaster haunted my life for forty-five years before I sat down and began to look carefully at the materials and consider how I might approach them. In 1998, I had just moved back to the west coast from a teaching position in Montreal, so I was able to visit the scene of the disaster, to drive and walk across the bridge. I could also think of interviewing some of the survivors, though I was nervous about intruding on their lives, forcing them to re-live those moments. So, with other books to finish, I hesitated, yet again.

Four years passed. I noticed in *BC Bookworld* a review of Tom Berger's memoir, *One Man's Justice: A Life in the Law,* which mentioned his defence of the ironworkers who had brought the rebuilt Second Narrows Bridge almost to completion before taking legal strike action. The strike was declared illegal. They had the choice of going back to work or facing contempt of court charges. Berger was one of my heroes for his work on the Mackenzie Valley Pipeline Inquiry, but this was a part of the bridge story I did not know. I purchased a copy at Munro's in Victoria and quickly located the chapter entitled "A Bridge Too Far."

This proved to be a turning-point in my research. I read Berger's account of defending the striking ironworkers under impossible circumstances, a neophyte lawyer facing a crusty old judge with a reputation for being conservative, short-tempered and hardly sympathetic to union members, most of whom were probably communists and agitators. Justice Manson was patronizing in the extreme, dismissing the young whippersnapper defending the workers' right to strike. Manson wanted them back on the job, claiming that the bridge was dangerous in its present condition. Doubtless, he was concerned about the interests of his cronies in Dominion Bridge and Swan Wooster & Associates, the consulting engineers. Berger politely pointed out that, if the bridge was unsafe for the citizens of Vancouver, it would be equally unsafe for the workers returning to the job. And, after all, your honour, it had already collapsed once. When Berger asked if he could quote from the Magna Carta, the old judge was dismissive: "Don't talk to me about the Magna Carta! I'm up to here with the Magna Carta." Berger managed to slip in his choice quotation: "No man is obliged to build bridges should he choose not to." The courtroom exploded with applause. Manson was furious.

      I met Tom Berger for lunch. He was still working, long after official retirement, and had offices in the Marine Building, one of my favourite structures in the city, an art deco affair with a fringe of icing around the roof that looks like snow. One of the tallest buildings in Vancouver when I was a boy, it is now dwarfed by huge towers, including the one next door where my daughter Bronwen was working for Environment Canada. Berger, lively and gracious, insisted on buying me lunch and offered to lend me his personal copy of the court proceedings, which arrived at my house at French Beach a day later by priority post, with the note: "Return this when you're finished. All of my stuff goes to the archives at UBC, in due course." Although the court case had taken place more than a year after the bridge collapse, it presented me with evidence of a continuing saga, with repercussions and, most importantly, the names and recorded comments (angry, ironic, deliberately uncooperative) of some of the surviving ironworkers.

Berger's enthusiasm for the project gave me the nudge I needed to make contact with the surviving ironworkers, but this might not have happened so quickly without the intervention of Tom Evans, a film-maker and social activist. Tom interviewed Berger a few weeks after I did and we were made aware of each other's existence and mutual interests. I called him from a cell phone at Ogden Point and asked if we could meet. "Where are you?" he inquired. "I'm on the beach at Kits," I said, adding that I was not far from the Maritime Museum. "I'll meet you at the dock there in ten minutes." As I stood on the dock checking out the antique vessels and several signs warning against illegal docking and unauthorized use of the floats, I heard my name shouted. Gliding between the breakwater and the float was a small fibreglass sloop with two figures in the stern, both waving. I grabbed a line amidships, stepped aboard and we were off again, introductions made over the noise of the outboard motor. After the sails were set, the intrepid Liam, Tom's charming seven-year-old son and first mate, disappeared into the cabin to play computer games.

Tom Evans, a short man with the heart of an Olympian, realized at once that I was out of my element, if not in the boat, at least in terms of how to proceed with my research and writing about the bridge disaster. So, he invited me to accompany him to the annual memorial service on June 17, 2005, where I met retired bridge foreman Lou Lessard, who gave a rousing speech to the assembled group; Donnie Geisser, whose father Charley had been operating the crane when the bridge collapsed; Charlie Guttmann, the son of Erich Guttmann who was arrested and jailed briefly during the subsequent strike; and Barrie Doyle, brought down from a job in Kelowna to help dismantle the bridge, and who would become the unofficial archivist of the disaster. After the speeches and the laying of wreaths at the memorial, a cement and marble monument containing the names of those killed on the bridge, several of us went out for beers to a familiar hangout on Hastings Street. These introductions were exactly what I needed. Now, not only were my feet wet, I was in the water—in the swim, as it were—and had better take the advice given to Conrad's Lord Jim, and let the "destructive element" bear me up.

Although I tape-recorded the interviews, I never had to go back and listen to the conversations I'd had with ironworkers, engineers, lawyers and union employees. The rhythms of their speech remained fixed in my mind and when I sat down at home to record my impressions, there was always a single story or event I'd been told that stood out and demanded attention. This was certainly the case with Barry Doyle's saga, where he described the near collapse of another bridge and compared it to being attacked by Jim English's wife Ruby in a beer parlour downtown.

Ladies & Escorts

I walked off a job in Castlegar
for safety reasons. Dismantling steel
is what we were doing, temporary
structures, so late in the day
you couldn't see bugger-all. I wanted
to quit. The foreman, gung-ho,
insisted there was plenty of light
to finish the job. Hundred and eighty feet
to the river. Couldn't swim a stroke.
We kept several bolts in place,
inserted a couple of pins to knock
out as the choker tightened
and the crane took up the weight.

Nobody calculated the wind-factor.
About to pop pins, when the beam
leans out over the river. A goner,
I thought, drowning in the pitch-
black, or flattened on rocks.
I screamed at the foreman.
He was running towards the crane,
only the white dot of his hard-hat
visible below. Wind and weight
had tilted the rig thirty degrees.
It tottered, tried to make up its mind.
Headlights. Auxiliary crane
barrelled downhill, hooked
onto the other, eased it back
into position. Get up, Doyle,
the foreman shouted next morning.
Fuck you, I quit. You can't do that,
it's not safe. It was less safe last night
when you almost got me killed. Another
close call was in the beer parlour
of the Biltmore Hotel downtown.
I called Jim English something nasty
and his wife Ruby came at me swinging.
I can still feel the wind as her punch
went wide of the mark. Decked me,
she would have. So help me, Jesus,
this is dangerous work.

Some of these stories required less tinkering than others. Of course, many of the men had experienced similar feelings as they fell from the bridge, so I had to alter their stories slightly to elicit the less rehearsed and seemingly extraneous details that make for a more intimate and moving utterance. After several months there were still large gaps in the narrative. At that point, fictional voices began to enter: a Vancouver lawyer whose father was killed on the bridge, an injured ironworker with a very different kind of story to tell, a woman trying to deal with her resentment at being widowed, a returning veteran who would have preferred the study of mushrooms, but took up ironwork instead. In several cases, the manufactured 'voice' felt more real, more authentic, to me than the ones I'd recorded, perhaps because I was not inhibited by fact or by a sense of responsibility to the individual whom I'd interviewed.

While the actors moved with consummate grace through their various roles, from brash ironworker to angry widow to lecherous son, I scanned the faces in the audience. Tom Berger must have sensed me looking at him, as he glanced in my direction and gave a discreet wave. As the performance unfolded, rain pattered on the corrugated metal roof of the machine-shop and water dripped here and there on the heads of the long-suffering audience. I was struck yet again by the subjectivity of history, the compromise, or series of comprises, that each writer makes with the past. Perhaps it would be more accurate to call the process of writing history a reconciliation—a private truth and reconciliation commission—that goes on in the head for so long that it emanates in a story or narrative, a perhaps vain attempt to grasp and explain a brief or extended moment in the private or collective past. Of course, that's never the end of the story. As soon as the historical moment has been inscribed, doubts emerge, new insights and information demand to be included, taken into account. Did it really happen that way? What have I left out? And those damned blinkers or dirty lenses. Could there be another way of looking at this event that draws entirely different conclusions? When I began to think seriously about the collapse of the Second Narrows Bridge, I had no idea what I wanted to say. All I knew was that the event had made a huge impression on that gangly teenager who had just graduated from high school and was hoping to make enough money during the summer to pay his university fees.

My mother had died in Vancouver when I was seven years old, so I was not unfamiliar with trauma and loss. The cancer that had taken her from me was yet another form of structural failure, less a matter of human error than of genetic deficiency. She, too, had been a bridge, an essential part of the support system that was to carry me from birth to adulthood, but a bridge with a flaw in the blueprint. Though I'm speculating here (still writing history), the collapse of the bridge brought that earlier loss back to mind, set me thinking about other families and their losses and their pain. I was not yet a writer, so I had no inkling that this event might figure in my later life other than as a vaguely troubling memory in a generally dysfunctional childhood.

By the time of writing, I'd read enough poetry, including Hart Crane's "The Bridge" and Adrienne Rich's fine poem "Diving into the Wreck," to be alerted to the welter of symbols in the swirling waters of the Second Narrows and to sense in that partially submerged memory more than a faint hint of possibility. A bridge, after all, is a metaphor, a carrying across; and the idea of poetry as rescue work, diving or digging into history, as into the self, would continue to tease me. Writing, too, I had to admit, is a form of *falsework*, a temporary support structure like that used to build bridges, something we depend on to take us part way towards the truth. I agreed with the great Italian critic Benedetto Croce: "Without narrative, there is no history." I had recorded and constructed a series of short poetic anecdotes, but still faced the problem of turning them into a convincing and provocative narrative or poem-sequence. I had a powerful event, I had a personal connection to that event, but still I did not have a successful narrative. I could see a story taking shape around the question: who was responsible for the bridge collapse? I could also imagine another story to be found in the experience of diving for bodies. Neither of these approaches seemed likely to capture the epicentre of the collapse—that moment and its terrible ramifications. I did not want a single over-riding narrative. I wanted to tell the story at a glance, *pris sur le vif,* as it were, through a series of mini-stories, so spare and intimate they would invite a reader only halfway into the room, providing a glimpse of an object, a mood, an angle of light, hinting rather than telling. But how to pull these diverse voices together?

While the bridge itself functioned almost as a character, or presence, in the book, I needed something else. That was when the writer and researcher began to assume a larger role in the unfolding story, a self-reflexive turn that enabled me to bring process—that is, the machinery of narration—into the foreground. While I ransacked some of my own life-material (a diver father, a drowned grandfather, an academic interview, an afternoon spent in the Vancouver archives), I happily fictionalised the rest, making the writer a journalist, a jazz aficionado, and letting him argue and spend an afternoon in the sack with a savvy lover who serves as a useful foil, and a very sensible counterpoint to his grumpy and negative pronouncements about life and art.

This process had its surprises, especially as the role of my father began to surface at regular intervals. His involvement with the bridge disaster had been useful in introducing myself to ironworkers, but no one I interviewed, including divers, remembered him or could verify his presence at the bridge on June 17, 1958 or any day thereafter. Had my father really been involved or had he cooked up the story for some private reason? As I restructured *Falsework*, my father and the notion of fathering assumed a larger significance, to the point where the manuscript ended with a meditation about truth and reliability, in art as in life, and with a very personal account of my father's death:

I recall standing at his deathbed ten years ago, holding his hand, watching the faint rise and fall of his chest and listening to the slow hiss of oxygen through the clear plastic mask on his face and the thin rubber hose connected to a stainless-steel cylinder attached to the bed-frame. The inscription on the label read: Breath of Life. The evening sky outside the basement apartment in Port Edward was, appropriately, salmon-pink for my diver, fisherman, truck-driver father, this man I worshipped but hardly knew, preparing his final descent, this time into the earth. True or false, I still can't say. However, as if by magic, and from the grave itself, he has once again managed to write me into his story, a bridge, a tenuous rope of narrative, along which I am moving, cautiously, one foot placed carefully in front of the other, every muscle, every breath contributing to my precarious balance.

It was not an ending I could have anticipated when I began writing *Falsework*, but it seemed to shift the question of responsibility—for safety, for honesty, for caring, for meticulous recording—from the anonymous institutions of government and corporations, back to the individuals who do the dirty work and who sign off on documents, including works of imagination.

* * *

There are other things happening in *Falsework* that might justify the book's claim, at least for me, to be poetry rather than prose documentary or merely a lesson in local history. If much contemporary fiction sounds and feels as if it were being written with the movies in mind, it's probably fair to say that much contemporary poetry is being written with performance, particularly the public reading, in mind, and with radio and theatre lurking in the wings. This, for me, is the great tradition of poetry, an oral art that originally used as much rhyme and metre and repetition as were necessary to make a work memorable and memorizable. I have enjoyed this new-found freedom, preferring to focus my attention on the rich rhythms of the speaking-voice in its story-telling or emotive states, and to concentrate on varying the pitch and acoustic density of the text from line to line and poem to poem. *Falsework* also embodies my conviction that poetry does not serve two opposing masters—the urge to sing and the urge to narrate—but, rather, is the form most appropriate for satisfying these two intimately related human impulses. An ancient Chinese scholar puts the emphasis where it belongs when he advises: *narrate as if singing and sing as if narrating*. Whether this not-so-newfangled poetic licence succeeds, or should be revoked and removed from the whale-road, only time will tell.

The dramatic rendition of *Falsework* by talented actors touched me profoundly. Survivors and families of victims were in the audience. The rain, miraculously, had stopped. When the lights came up a middle-aged man and woman in the front row were wiping away tears. An attractive and elegantly dressed older woman approached me after the performance to say she was the widow of the young Australian engineer John McKibbin who died when the bridge collapsed and who, in my version of events, had been wrongly blamed for a mathematical error that contributed to the disaster. She wanted to thank me for lifting an enormous weight from her shoulders. I gave her a hug and said I wished I'd written the book years earlier.

That night the work of art and the art of work fused into a single project for me, giving me a deeper sense of solidarity with the world of labour, white collar and blue. There would be other pleasures in store later, when *Falsework* was set to music by composer Larry Nickel and sung by the Vancouver Chamber Choir; when it was featured on Sounds Like Canada and then listed in the *Globe and Mail* by CBC host Shelagh Rogers as her "favourite book of the year"; and when Montreal composer Tim Brady announced his intention to use it as the basis of a symphony for multiple choirs. But nothing could match those moments in the machine-shop at Ocean Cement Company. As *Falsework* and I made our way across the country, I was continually reminded that poetry not only has the potential for healing on an individual level, but also that its music and intimacy can work their magic at a broad public level.

7: Gary Geddes: The Writer as Witness

[*Born in Vancouver, Gary Geddes lives at French Beach on Vancouver Island, but has taught and lectured at universities across Canada and sojourned abroad. He has written and edited more than 35 books, including the bestselling memoir,* Sailing Home, *and won over a dozen national and international awards, among them the Americas Best Book Award and the Gabriela Mistral Prize. A prolific poet, Geddes is the author of sixteen volumes of poetry, including the memorable* Skaldance, *and the translator (with George Liang) of* I Didn't Notice the Mountain Growing Dark: Poems of Li Bai and Du Fu. *Most recently, he was Distinguished Professor of Canadian Culture in the Center for Canadian-American Studies at Western Washington University in Bellingham, and is the current writer-in-residence at the Vancouver Public Library. As a mentor and as a writer, Geddes conveys a humane perspective on issues both personal and political, whether documenting the world's forgotten places and histories, or exploring his own family legends. His nonfiction writing, as evidenced in* The Kingdom of Ten Thousand Things, *incorporates history, political analysis and cultural anthropology in an eloquent call to arms. Here, in conversation with Fernanda Viveiros, he speaks on the paradox of living in the twenty-first century.*]

Fernanda Viveiros: You've served as a writer-in-residence at numerous universities including the University of Alberta, Malaspina University College, the University of Ottawa and Green College at UBC. How different is it for you to work with members of the public—as opposed to students—in your present position as the writer-in-residence at the Vancouver Public Library?

Gary Geddes: Working with members of the public is always less exhausting than working with students. The students are mostly very committed, have paid hard cash for the privilege of picking brains, and are also often, though not always, fairly well versed in literature and criticism. So, it can be quite demanding to work with serious creative writing students who want and deserve the best you can give them. People who visit a writer-in-residence at the library may be just as serious as their university counterparts, but they are often less demanding and more grateful for whatever you can offer in terms of time and constructive criticism. I usually ask for short manuscripts, about five pages, which allows me to give those pages fairly detailed attention. The reading takes an hour, writing a solid one- or two-page critique takes at least an hour, and meeting with the student takes another hour, so the whole process involves quite a commitment. There's nothing like the pleasure of seeing a light come on in a writer's face when something that may be quite obvious to me is pointed out—a different way to break the line, the kind of torque that can be generated by enjambment, ways to increase density of image and sound in a poem, altering the patterns of stressed and unstressed syllables.

FV: Christopher Hitchens believes there is a direct link between musical and literary talent and I'm reminded by your comment above—about the "sound in a poem"—that you've said you often sang as a child.

GG: I think it's true that poets with musical training, like Robyn Sarah and Jan Zwicky, are more likely to find the music in language early in their careers. For the rest of us, it takes a little longer. I had no musical training as a child, but I listened to the radio and sang at the top of my lungs while weeding two acres of potatoes. I had a good ear and memory for tunes. Later, I sang in a church choir and a rock group called The High Fives. The 'high' had nothing to do with narcotic substances, but with the fact that we were high school students and high on music. One guitar and five voices. We did everything from "Blue Suede Shoes" to "In the Jungle," with me taking the high tenor parts. I think music could have been an alternative career for me had domestic penury not prevented me from studying the subject. Joseph Conrad spoke of writing as a form that aspires "to the magic suggestiveness of music," which is something I've struggled with throughout my career. The two dominant impulses in poetry are lyric and narrative, the pull of story and the pull of song. As a writer of long poems and narratives, my concern has been to achieve enough moments of lyric intensity in my work to lift it above conventional prose. This involves knowing how to break the lines, how to vary patterns of stress and how to make enough happen in terms of recurring sound to give seemingly ordinary speech a touch of magic and grace.

FV: Was your own early writing shaped by a literary mentor?

GG: I had no single literary mentor. However, I had the good fortune to be asked to edit two anthologies, one national and one international, when I was still wet behind the poetic ears. This forced me to read widely and deeply in order to figure out what certain poets were trying to achieve, how they were getting certain effects in their work. As a result, I made a huge commitment of time and energy studying the works of 50 to 100 very fine poets. The conception and scope of both anthology projects demanded that I have something useful and original to say about each of these poets, without interfering with a student's efforts to understand and interpret the poem. This was a great challenge and most of the time I was flying by the seat of my pants trying to live up to my own and Oxford's expectations. So, I owe my modest achievements to a host of very fine writers, many of them Canadian. The thing is, you never stop learning, and always seem to be starting again from scratch.

FV: Although well known as a political poet, two of your more recent titles have been works of non-fiction: *Sailing Home: A Journey Through Time, Place and Memory* and another travel memoir, *The Kingdom of Ten Thousand Things*. Here again, you are inspired by your travels, by your exposure to both foreign and familiar territory—and yet you've said you travel "in order to escape the vortex of subjectivity, to get away from home where the whirl of self in the static world left me dizzy, unsettled." Are you saying you feel more at peace, even more substantial, when travelling?

GG: No, I'm not more at peace travelling. In fact, I am quite a nervous traveller, always over-awed by the spectacle of cultures so different from my own and by the simple tasks of finding a cheap bed and reliable food. I think I was trying to suggest that the self in stasis needs a regular shaking up, to avoid complacency, egotism, and all the perils of thinking one's own lot is somehow the template for humanity. I was very fortunate as an academic to have a regular income, a modicum of social status, and time to spare. I know a lot of shit is happening in the world out there. At times I feel I must immerse myself in that more troubled stream, live cheaply, stick my neck out, take some risks, and try to understand at the grassroots level what is happening in more troubled places.

FV: Your writing often addresses "personal and tribal ghosts" as you touch upon the mystical, the religious, the sainthood found in the lives of common people. In one interview, you even say that as a youth you wanted to be a preacher and save the world. Is exposing and recording the world's "sins" via your poems, prose and memoir akin to confession? Is there some sense of guilt in not being able to heal or fix all those things you have witnessed in your travels?

GG: It was not out of pure whimsy that nineteenth-century writer Cardinal Newman called his autobiography *Apologia Pro Vita Sua*. All writing, all art, is an apology for our failed lives. We write so that others might love us, or at least understand us, and hopefully love themselves a little more in the process. Bronwen Wallace spoke a lot about Lao Tzu and his notion that we should address the wound in each other, the part that is broken, damaged, in ruins. By addressing this wound, this breakage, we declare our affinity and solidarity with others. I don't need to go to Gaza or Nicaragua or Chile to know that suffering is the daily bread for much of humanity; Hastings and Main in downtown Vancouver will do. I am interested in understanding the reasons for this suffering and my own complicity.

FV: Many poets, especially those from South and Central America, Asia and parts of Europe, have had a strong political commitment, both in their lives and in their poetry. Your writing is dangerous—or would be, if you actually lived in a country where journalists and writers are routinely tortured or shot.

GG: I've spent time on the barricades, and working on the left: I was an active protestor against the Vietnam War; I interviewed Vietnamese boat people in Hong Kong camps; I went to Chile during the Pinochet dictatorship to do human rights interviews; I was in Nicaragua during the Sandinista regime, protesting with Kris Kristofferson in front of the US embassy against American support of the Contras; I travelled to Gaza, West Bank and Israel after the Oslo Accord to monitor the situation there; and I was in Afghanistan on a Taliban visa two weeks before 9/11 after spending two weeks interviewing Afghan refugees in camps in Pakistan. Inequality and inequity trouble me. None of this work was driven, I hope, by perverse or grandiose motives. I simply felt concerned and was moved to learn more about these trouble sites. I doubt that my poems and prose about Chile or Palestine or Central America have saved any lives, though they have named names and pointed to deficiencies in myself and in the cultures that have shaped and sustained me. I'm grateful for the conditions that enable me to travel and write about what I see as honestly as I can, but I'm always conscious of the hypocrisy here that allows us to masquerade as international peacekeepers abroad while, at home, we slaughtered the Beothuk Indians, robbed and degraded other First Nations, imprisoned our Japanese-Canadians, taxed and treated as second-rate our Chinese-Canadians, turned away a shipload of European Jews fleeing the Holocaust, inflicted the War Measures Act on the Quebecois.

FV: You're not the first Canadian writer to take to the seas after the implosion of a relationship or career but in your case, rather than travel someplace warm or exotic, you chose your own back yard: the west coast of BC. In *Sailing Home: A Journey Through Time, Place and Memory* you write of navigating "in a sea teeming with personal and tribal ghosts." Which came first, the idea for the book — or the need to escape?

GG: Neither. I was a fledgling sailor, descended from a long line of Scottish fishermen and boat builders. As a child, I gillnetted with my father in Rivers Inlet; later, I worked at my uncle's boat rentals in Howe Sound and drove water taxi during the summer when I taught school on Texada Island. I think I can claim a few grains of salt in my blood. I owned a sailboat years earlier when I taught at the University of Victoria, so it had been a long-time ambition of mine to own a decent boat and sail up the coast. When I proposed writing a memoir about the coast, my editor Phyllis Bruce at HarperCollins reminded me that memoirs are written by important people, not schmucks. Phyllis was a friend, so she could get away with the hard truth. I had to agree. My life seemed important to me, but I could not imagine it would seem important enough to anyone else to justify a whole book. So I suggested to Phyllis that I would tack back and forth between the personal and the public, between sailing and reminiscence. I think I convinced her that my drowned grandfather, my aunt with the wooden leg, and my uncle who had bombed and been shot down over Hamburg were not exactly bland materials for a memoir. Writing *Sailing Home* was not escape; it was a salvage operation. I was recovering family history and giving imaginative shape to vanishing legends, mine and yours.

FV: This sense of wanting to connect to the past, to reveal the hidden, is present in much of your writing, and especially so with *The Kingdom of Ten Thousand Things* where you attempt to follow in the footsteps of Huishen, a fifth-century Buddhist monk who you believe may have had contact with the native people of North America's west coast. Did your travels through Afghanistan, China and Mexico lead you to any firm conclusions?

GG: No graffiti was found saying "Huishen was here." A Chinese scholar of Buddhism I met had never heard of him; neither had the citizens of Jingzhou, the walled city in China, where he is said to have made his report to the emperor and court historians and, later, been buried. Though Huishen remained elusive and his trail uncertain, I certainly found enough interesting material to make me question the traditional Bering land-bridge theory of the peopling of the Americas and to believe that Asian contact with the Americas has been happening for thousands of years, most of it by way of coastal migration. I share the conclusions of David Kelly and Betty Meggers, two archaeologists who, respectively, consider the ocean not a barrier but a conveyor-belt and a superhighway. Most important, I think, was the lesson embedded in all of this frenetic travel and research: we are all interconnected, part of the same family, and there is no barrier, however arduous or distant, that humans, out of curiosity or desperation, will not attempt to cross.

FV: A translator yourself, a number of your own books have been translated into Chinese, Dutch, French, Italian, Spanish and Portuguese. How closely did you work with the translators? Were variations made to the text in any of these versions in order to adjust for cultural differences?

GG: Translation is a wonderful art, one for which I have the greatest respect. I wish Canadians did more of it and Canada Council felt inclined to support it. And yet there are always surprises when a text is translated. Australian poet Chris Wallace-Crabbe once told me about receiving the page-proofs for the Italian translation of his poems. He found they had translated the word 'nappies' (the Australian term for diapers) as 'little sleeps.'

I do not know other languages well enough to contribute significantly to the translation process, so I have had to take it all on faith. I was startled to find that my run-on couplets in *The Terracotta Army* had been changed into closed couplets in the Chinese version, making them seem more traditional to a Chinese reader. Frost says that poetry is what is lost in the translation. However, I am convinced that much is found, too, in the process. Perhaps the greatest discovery is that a microscopic study of someone else's poem brings us back to language at its most intimate, its most basic—the intricate patterning of image, sound and idea.

FV: Saramago has said, "the job of poetry, its political job, is to refresh the idea of justice, which is going dead in us all the time." In your own writing, you often touch upon the misuse of power, and the "dark side" of politics, religion and culture. What drives you to record the violent images you see and how do you reconcile its existence in the twenty-first century with your own belief in justice?

GG: My eldest daughter Jenny, who teaches at the University of Virginia and edits *The Hedgehog Review*, writes about evil and is a specialist in Holocaust writing. She spends a lot of time thinking about this question which troubles me so deeply, so perhaps there's something in the genes, all those Scottish genes shaped by too much oatmeal and the outrage of Culloden and the Clearances. The things that trouble me—and the voices in the past that cry out to be written down—have to be given imaginative shape, a verbal home. That seems to be my way of shaking off the albatross of Kent State, the Disappeared of Chile, the Spanish Conquest, displaced Palestinians. I don't invent the violence; and I certainly don't celebrate it. My own pain matters to me, but it does not matter in the grand scheme of things. I don't write to tell people how sad or hurt I am. I write to make them feel those events long after the fact, to keep certain terrible moments alive in the imagination, on record. While there is often no justice, there is always the potential for hope. When the poem works, as Yeats said, "a terrible beauty is born."

FV: I understand your new book, *Falsework*, is described as an "illustrated, book-length poetic narrative," is based on the Second Narrows Bridge tragedy in 1958. This event had personal significance for you in that your father was involved in the search for bodies in the water. Was this the first time you attempted to write about the bridge collapse?

GG: Yes, I'd been thinking about that event sporadically for almost fifty years, since the bridge came down during construction June 17, 1958, the month I graduated from King Edward High School. It's been a long gestation period. I don't recommend waiting that long, since so many of the men I might have spoken to had already passed away, but I had no choice: I was not ready emotionally or physically for the task.

FV: In addition to being a literary mentor, editor, critic and active promoter of Canadian writers, your career has included stints as the publisher of Quadrant Editions and Cormorant Books. Given your long career in Canadian publishing and having worked on both sides of the fence, what do you feel are the biggest challenges facing this country's publishing industry?

GG: The biggest challenge continues to be how to survive as an independent country next-door to the United States. Despite all the claptrap about living in a global village, television, internet and new media have a homogenizing effect, an Americanizing effect. So our publishing and other arts will need even greater financial support if we are to stand against the tsunami of American books and magazines and movies and television programs threatening to engulf us. Fortunately, our best writers and artists are forging a distinctly Canadian consciousness that is being recognized abroad, even though many Canadians at home are not even aware of what is happening. Is the survival of Canada as an independent state as important a concern as the survival of the planet? It's exciting to think of the link between these two issues and the possibility that we might, as Canadians, become part of a global solution rather than part of the continuing problem.

8: Letter from the Grand Canyon

I am a poet. I do other things to make a living. I teach classes and edit books; I've also been a publisher, a warehouseman, a fishing guide and a water-taxi driver. But my primary concern is always to write poems. Writing poems is not a task that pays very well, as Ezra Pound has reminded us (I once received a royalty cheque for 16 cents Canadian!); and it's not a task that brings much recognition in this world of fast-food and information-overload. As Don Marquis, the American author of *Archie & Mehitabel*, says: "Publishing a book of poems is like dropping a rose petal into Grand Canyon and waiting to hear the echo." Canadian artist A.Y. Jackson expressed a similar sentiment when he insisted that his countrymen would rather support a boa constrictor than a poet. When was the last time you saw someone in a restaurant or on a bus reading a book of poems? How often do you see poems published or reviewed in newspapers? Even in English departments at universities, where they ought to know better, many academics avoid poetry. They think of it as something difficult and arcane, easily set aside for the sweep and popular appeal of the novel.

And yet poetry, for all of society's indifference to it, is central to all of our lives. It's a verdict, a call to arms, a message from the heart, an urgent final communication. Nobel laureate Czeslaw Milosz believes that poetry is as essential as bread. Octavio Paz, another Nobel laureate, insists that "a society without poetry is a society without dreams." Poetry connects us with the primary process experiences of birth, infancy and early childhood, those moments when we were learning to navigate, when we gave up our watery refuge for the perilous world of burning oxygen, where we had to cope with a deluge of unfamiliar sounds and signals, where the utterances we heard and tried to imitate were so intimately tied to the basic rhythms of life, to the heart-beat, to the thrum of blood in the brain, to the cycles of feeding, sleep and elimination. We spent a lot of waking time exercising our vocal chords, sometimes by crying or screaming, but also by sucking syllables, clicking consonants, forming words that would express how we felt and, perhaps, get us what we wanted.

Some of these linguistic games were magical. They had nothing to do with the secondary language of communication which we call prose, where everything comes out sounding logical and in subordinate and coordinate clauses. In poetry, which I call our first language, we had no trouble as small children imagining cows jumping over the moon or a dish running away for clandestine weekends in Bellingham with a spoon. We could not analyze these texts, but we loved and revelled in their sounds and we could visualize their images, take pleasure in their strange leaps and juxtapositions. Deep in our being we still associate poetry with those early pleasures; somehow poetry helped us endure the painful and inevitable separation from our mother's body, our gradual displacement from the comfort of the breast and the security of the family. And it has the power to help us through all the joys, the high drama, and the displacements to come.

My five-year-old grandson Jeremy, not a very enthusiastic eater at the best of times, was sitting at the supper-table day-dreaming when his mother's older friend Cameron, in exasperation, said: "Jeremy you're really weird." Jeremy looked quite puzzled for a moment, not quite knowing how to process this information. Then he looked up at Cameron and said: "Sometimes I'm weird, sometimes I'm not." This little symmetrical structure pleased him immensely and he could be heard throughout the afternoon expanding his repertoire: "Sometimes I'm lucky, sometimes I'm not; sometimes I'm purple, sometimes I'm green." He had created a rhythmical construct to help him ward off adult aggression; he was using poetic techniques to shape and control his world. Whether or not you agree with Margaret Atwood that poetry is the "heart of language," it's the music poems embody that touches us, that nests in the ear and works its magic.

During the Vietnam war, when the Ohio National Guard opened fire on the unarmed students at Kent State University, killing four of them and wounding nine others, I found myself in a state of great confusion. I could make no sense of what was happening; my grief and rage and frustration demanded some sort of resolution, some poetic shape. I tried unsuccessfully for six years to write a poem that would put to rest these demons. Then one day I walked into a bookstore in Edmonton and found on the shelf a small paperback volume by the great American journalist I.F. Stone, who was one voice you could trust in the media; it was called *The Killings at Kent State* and it tried to understand what had happened and why no members of the military had ever been brought to trial for these killings. As I walked home with this little red book, which cost me a dollar, I noticed four details that galvanized my attention about one of the victims, a girl named Sandra Lee Scheuer: she was a speech therapy student, she was very tidy, she loved to roller-skate, and she knew nothing about politics. Somehow the time was right and the necessary materials were at hand, so I chucked my previous efforts and sat down to write. This is what came to me.

SANDRA LEE SCHEUER

(Killed at Kent State University on May 4, 1970
by the Ohio National Guard)

You might have met her on a Saturday night
cutting precise circles, clockwise, at the Moon-Glo
Roller Rink, or walking with quick step

between the campus and a green two-storey house,
where the room was always tidy, the bed made,
the books in confraternity on the shelves.

She did not throw stones, major in philosophy
or set fire to buildings, though acquaintances say
she hated war, had heard of Cambodia.

In truth she wore a modicum of make-up, a brassiere,
and could, no doubt, more easily have married a guardsman
than cursed or put a flower in his rifle barrel.

While the armouries burned she studied,
bent low over notes, speech therapy books, pages
open at sections on impairment, physiology.

And while they milled and shouted on the commons
she helped a boy named Billy with his lisp, saying
Hiss, billy, like a snake. That's it, SSSSSSSS,

tongue well up and back behind your teeth.
Now buzz, Billy, like a bee. Feel the air
vibrating in my windpipe as I breathe?

As she walked in sunlight through the parking-lot
at noon, feeling the world a passing lovely place,
a young guardsman, who had his sights on her,

was going down on one knee as if he might propose.
His declaration, unmistakable, articulate,
flowered within her, passed through her neck,

severed her trachea, taking her breath away.
Now who will burn the midnight oil for Billy,
ensure the perilous freedom of his speech?

And who will see her skating at the Moon-Glo
Roller Rink, the eight small wooden wheels
making their countless revolutions on the floor?

If there is one more urgent final communication I can share with you, it's this. Keep yourself open to experience, particularly poetic experience. I am not speaking here only about words on the page. Karl Shapiro once described poetry as a way of *seeing* things, not just a way of saying things. We all possess the poetic faculty; it's that which enables us to intuit, to sense beauty and danger, to see through to the essence of a person, an event, an emotion. Written and spoken poetry slows things down, makes us conscious of time in its passage; it anchors us to the moment by appealing to our senses. It's our way of naming and celebrating and shaping our world, giving it, as Conrad says, the permanence of memory.

When I was young, I tried to write poems to get the attention and win the hearts of young women. Unfortunately, these poems opened no doors for me. I had not taken the time to learn the craft or to give my full attention to the beloved. Only later did I learn that all good poems, whatever their subject-matter, are love-poems. They speak, first, of our love of the language; then they speak of our love for the things of this world in all their glory and tatters. Ted Hughes described poems, not inaccurately, as urgent communications that have the character of "ragged dirty undated letters from remote battles and weddings."

Poetry, in other words, is a way of being in love with the creatures and the forms of this earth. And the earth and its atmosphere and its peoples need nothing more, at this point in history, than the loving attention of the poet in each one of you.

Acknowledgements

Some of these essays appeared in the following books and literary and magazines: "Country Music" was published in *The British Journal of Commonwealth Literature*, Volume Twelve, Number One; "Going the Distance" first appeared in *Open Letter,* Long Liners Conference Issue, Nos. 2-3, Summer-Fall 1985; an abbreviated version of "Bridging the Narrows" appeared in *The Capilano Review*; "The Long Poem As Potlatch" appeared in as "Making Ars Longer" in *Books in Canada*; "The Machinery of Desire" first appeared under a different title in *Bolder Flights: Essays on the Canadian Long Poem*, edited by Frank Tierney and Angela Arnold Robbeson; "The Writer as Witness," an interview conducted by Fernanda Viveiros, was published in *Wordworks*. My thanks to the editors of these journals. Versions of the talk "A Letter from the Grand Canyon" were given at the University of Iowa and Royal Roads University.

The Mackie Lecture and Reading Series

In 2003, the KIWW, in association with Okanagan College and the Mackie Lake House Foundation, made available a writing residency. Dr. Ronald Ayling, Professor Emeritus, University of Alberta, was the first resident. Each year thereafter, a writer has combined a public lecture or reading with classroom visits, engagement with the community and the creation of a text. Neither genre nor subject matter is prescribed; the Mackie Residents have an unfettered mandate. The results, by year of residence, are:

2003:   Ronald Ayling, *Sean O'Casey's Theatre of War*, with a Preface by Craig McLuckie (0-9693482-7-4).

2004:   Dennis Cooley, *Country Music: New Poems*, with an Introduction by John Lent (0-9693482-8-2).

2005:   David Pitt-Brooke and Christine McPhee, *Accommodation: A Dialogue of Culture and Nature*, with an Introduction by Ann McKinnon (0-9738057-3-0).

2006:   Robert Kroetsch and John Lent, *Abundance: The Mackie House Conversations About the Writing Life*, with an Introduction by Sean Johnston (978-0-97380574-1).

2007:   Dawne McCance, *Sleights of Hand Derrida Writing* (978-0-9738057-6-5).

2008:   Gary Geddes, *Out of the Ordinary: meditations on poetry and narrative*, with an Introduction by Jake Kennedy (978-0-9738057-8-9).

2009: Mona Fertig, poet and publisher is the resident.

2010: Peter Midgely, academic, poet and editor will be the resident.